Teachers' Guide for

RELIGIOUS ISSUES IN AMERICAN CULTURE

**ROBERT A. SPIVEY
EDWIN S. GAUSTAD
RODNEY F. ALLEN**

Contributing Editor: Lawrence R. Hepburn

Addison-Wesley Publishing Company
Menlo Park, California • Reading, Massachusetts • London • Don Mills, Ontario

ISSUES IN RELIGION

Religious Issues in American Culture

Religious Issues in Western Civilization

Religious Issues in World Cultures

General Editors

Robert A. Spivey
Department of Religion
Florida State University, Tallahassee

Edwin S. Gaustad
Department of History
University of California, Riverside

Rodney F. Allen
Department of Social Studies Education
Florida State University, Tallahassee

Copyright © 1972 by Addison-Wesley Publishing Company, Inc.
Philippines Copyright 1972.

All rights reserved. No part of this publication may be reproduced, stored in a retrieval system, or transmitted, in any form or by any means, electronic, mechanical, photocopying, recording, or otherwise, without the prior written permission of the publisher. Printed in the United States of America. Published simultaneously in Canada.
ISBN 0-201-07099-5
BCDEFGHIJ–EB–7876543

CONTENTS

General Preface iv
Preface to Teachers iv
Basic Library vii
Correlation of Religious Issues in American Culture with Leading Social Studies Textbooks . . . ix
Study 1. Why Go to the New World? 1
Study 2. Conformity or Diversity? 16
Study 3. The American Revolution: A Religious War?. 28
Study 4. Subsidy or Separation? 36
Study 5. The Churches on the American Frontier 48
Study 6. Blacks and the Churches 64
Study 7. Religion: Personal and Social 80
Study 8. Ways of Understanding: Science and Religion 94
Study 9. Conscience or Constitution? 104
Study 10. America: Protestant or Pluralist?. 113

GENERAL PREFACE

In 1965 the Superintendent of Public Instruction for the State of Florida appointed a twelve-member "State Committee on Study About Religion in the Public Schools." This representative committee of citizens, wholly agreeable to the U.S. Supreme Court's proscriptions regarding the practice of religion in the public schools, began investigating constructive approaches to the study of religion in public schools. In 1968 a grant from the Danforth Foundation (St. Louis, Missouri) enabled a three-year curriculum project in social studies to get underway.

Social Studies, as already taught in the existing curriculum, of course cannot and does not avoid all mention of religion. For a variety of reasons, however, religion is rarely dealt with directly or in any appreciable depth. One of those reasons is that objective, pedagogically sound curriculum materials in this entire area of human experience have been conspicuously absent. The Religion-Social Studies Curriculum Project, based at Florida State University, therefore took this deficiency in published materials as its challenge and its task. Units were written for courses in American history, world history, developing nations, cultural geography and "problems of American democracy" (or "American studies").

Two generously funded summer institutes for high school teachers (in 1969 and 1970) provided ample opportunity for discussion, evaluation, and revision of the units. Also extensive field testing, inside the State of Florida and across the nation, preceded the final drafting of materials in their present form.

The three-volume series, "Issues in Religion," utilizing an inquiry approach, places primary source materials in the hands of the student. With appropriate editorial comment, questions for consideration, suggested activities and other aids, the student is not being "told about religion" he is learning about religion. And learning in a way that helps him make judgments, perceive values, and reach new levels of understanding. An extensive Teachers' Guide assists the classroom instructor in planning a mutually enriching experience.

The three volumes in this series are Religious Issues in American Culture, Religious Issues in Western Civilization, and Religious Issues in World Culture. It is the earnest hope of the general editors that all three volumes will contribute to a better understanding of the role of religion in the shaping of societies and in the experience of mankind.

Volume I which launches this series took its initial form in 1968-69, the first year that the Religion-Social Studies Curriculum Project was funded by the Danforth Foundation. Special acknowledgment is here made to the Danforth Foundation for its generosity and its continued encouragement. Acknowledgment is also made to Lawrence R. Hepburn who spent that year heavily involved in the Project's many undertakings.

PREFACE TO TEACHERS

RATIONALE

Any defensible program of teaching about religion in the social studies must meet certain criteria. The content of the material must be socially significant and suitable to the classroom. The teaching strategy must be such as to promote genuine learning, taking every safeguard to prevent indoctrination. Only then is the public school teacher warranted—legally or morally—in undertaking an examination in depth of religious issues in the heritage of man.

Each of the ten studies herein has an integrity of its own. In order to promote objectivity, it is important that any study chosen be used in its entirety. If pro's and con's are being presented in the primary sources—as they often are—it would clearly be a distortion to use only one segment of a study. It is not necessary that these studies be used in a fixed sequence, for they do not build upon one another. But it is necessary, we repeat, that any study selected be used as a whole, not in part.

Free inquiry and induction are characteristic of the materials. Students are asked to analyze source materials related to issues in religion and the social studies. On the basis of the information provided, students are asked to develop their own positions. Then an open, informed class discussion permits students to present their own findings, offer and defend their own points of view, and—above all—consider respectfully alternative positions than the one which they (or even the class as a whole) have reached.

Most discussion will be open-ended: that is, the class will not in unison arrive at "right" answers. Complex religion-social issues, either of the past or of the present, are not readily or permanently resolved. Successful class discussion requires that students be willing to hear and appreciate the viewpoints of fellow students. Members of the class should also learn to withhold final judgments when the information at hand is incomplete or fragmentary. Needless to say, the example set by the teacher in these matters is of the highest importance.

Rather than a mere fountain of facts, the teacher acts as a guide in learning. Because of the special importance of religion in the lives of many people, the teacher has an urgent responsibility to see that the freedom of each student's conscience is preserved and respected—on all sides. The teacher must create an atmosphere of free and open inquiry, making certain that a learning situation never deteriorates into intimidation or descends into indoctrination. Students should likewise be encouraged to prefer careful and thoughtful analysis to hasty judgments or authoritative opinions.

OBJECTIVES

Each study in this teachers' guide begins with a statement of that lesson's primary goals. In many cases the specific objectives will fall into line with the more general objectives already being pursued in your regular course. On occasion, the objectives can with profit be discussed with the students. At the end of a study, students may help evaluate the attainment of the goals in knowledge, skill and attitudes.

PLAN OF THE STUDIES

1. Introduction. Generally each study begins with a section designed to relate the central theme to the student's own experience or interest. The intent is to draw the student into a position where he is ready to meet the primary sources in an appropriate frame of mind.

2. Readings. The heart of each lesson consists of primary sources: letters, essays, diatribes, sermons, memoirs, judicial decisions, and the like. Because these are critical to the study, teachers should help students reach as complete an understanding as possible. To assist in this purpose, each reading is accompanied by guiding questions. These are not designed primarily as a basis for general discussion; rather, their aim is to help students extract important information from the reading. These questions will be doubly helpful if teachers use them in a supervised-study situation. The teachers' guide for each study includes information to be considered in responding to the guiding questions.

3. Contemporary Parallel. Long before the word "relevance" became a tiresome cliche, Alfred North Whitehead declared that ideas must be put to use. The educated citizen does not merely parrot

what he has learned; he applies his new knowledge to the problems of society and of men. Regarding the mind as merely a vessel to be filled or as an inert instrument to be sharpened is, said this remarkable philosopher-mathematician, "one of the most fatal, erroneous and dangerous conceptions ever introduced into the theory of education." He added: "The mind is never passive; it is a perpetual activity, delicate, receptive, responsive to stimulus. You cannot postpone its life until you have sharpened it. Whatever interest attaches to your subject matter must be evoked here and now; whatever powers you are strengthening in the pupil, must be exercised here and now; whatever possibilities of mental life your teaching should impart, must be exhibited here and now. That is the golden rule of education, and a very difficult one to follow. . . . There is only one subject matter for education, and that is Life in all its manifestations" (A. N. Whitehead, The Aims of Education, New York, 1929; Mentor Edition, p. 18).

This is the argument for the contemporary parallel, and properly utilized or explored its rewards are many. The teacher should, of course, feel free to introduce even more contemporary parallels from daily events coinciding with the actual presentation of the study.

4. Activities. The teachers' guide suggests both oral and written activities that may be presented at the conclusion of each study. In pursuing these activities, students should learn that their process of thinking is more important than any artificial agreement on "right" answers for all. Class discussion becomes a vehicle for developing fuller understanding of the major themes; it also gives students an opportunity to share their own findings and tentative conclusions. In such a situation teachers can evaluate the degree to which individual students are reaching the objectives set forth in the study. Written activities, in addition to providing a further basis of evaluation, enable the student to use his independent judgment and to develop his own positions more fully.

The "Suggestions for Further Research" require investigation beyond the limits of the material given to each student. In looking over the Resource Guide provided you may determine which research assignments are most feasible in your own community or school. As much as possible, such research tasks should be in response to student interest and initiative.

A word list which concludes each lesson makes it possible for students gradually to increase their own working vocabulary. By careful attention to the context in which each word is used, it is often possible to arrive at a satisfactory understanding of the meaning of the word. Routine assignments in the dictionary should be avoided.

RESOURCE GUIDE

At the conclusion of each study you will find a listing of resources that may prove useful to you in a variety of ways. Some may be useful chiefly in broadening your own background or understanding. Others may be useful chiefly to the students, especially in the independent assignments or in seeking answers to questions raised in their own minds. Some of the resources are best consulted before the study, some best used as a part of the study (e.g., the films), and still others have their greatest utility at the conclusion of the class investigation. It is most appropriate therefore, that you look over the Resource Guide well in advance of the time that the material is to be used in class. All films should be previewed before showing to students. All books listed are currently in print; if they are unavailable locally, you may wish to order some of them directly from the publishers. All magazine articles are in periodicals commonly (though, of course, not universally) found in libraries.

Finally, the editors of this curriculum suggest a "Basic Library" on religion American culture. Your library should acquire as many of these volumes as is possible.

BASIC LIBRARY FOR RELIGION-SOCIAL STUDIES

Abell, Aaron. American Catholicism and Social Action. University of Notre Dame Press. $1.95.

Ahlstrom, S. E. A Religious History of the American People. Yale University Press. N.P.

Brauer, J. C. Protestantism in America. Westminster, revised edition. $3.95.

Burr, N. R. Religion in American Life. Appleton-Century-Crofts. $2.75.

Clark, E. T. The Small Sects in America. Abingdon Press, revised edition. $1.25.

Clebsch, W. A. From Sacred to Profane America. Harper. $5.95.

Cogley, John (ed.). Religion in America. Meridian (World). $2.25.

Ellis, J. T. American Catholicism. University of Chicago Press, revised edition. $2.95.

Ellis, J. T. Documents of American Catholic History. Regnery. 2 vols. $2.25 ea.

Frazier, E. F. Negro Church in America. Schocken. $1.45.

Gaustad, E. S. Historical Atlas of Religion in America. Harper. $8.95.

Gaustad, E. S. A Religious History of America. Harper. $8.95.

Gilbert, A. A Jew in Christian America. Sheed and Ward. $4.95.

Glazer, Nathan. American Judaism. University of Chicago Press. $1.95.

Gleason, Philip. Catholicism in America. Harper. $3.25.

Goldman, A. J. Giants of Faith: Great American Rabbis. Citadel Press. $6.95.

Handy, R. T. A Christian America. Oxford University. $7.95.

Harstein, J. I. (ed.) The Jews in American History. Anti-Defamation League, B'nai B'rith. $1.50.

Hudson, W. S. American Protestantism. University of Chicago Press. $1.95.

Hudson, W. S. Religion in America. Scribner's. $4.50.

Lurie, Rose G. American Jewish Heroes. Union of American Hebrew Congregations. $2.50.

McLoughlin, W. G. Modern Revivalism: Charles Grandison Finney to Billy Graham. Ronald Press. $6.50.

McLoughlin, W. G. and Bellah, R. N. Religion in America. Beacon. $3.45.

Marty, M. E. Righteous Empire. Dial Press. $7.95.

Mead, Frank S. Handbook of Denominations in the United States. Abingdon Press, revised edition. $2.95.

Basic Library for Religion–Social Studies

Mead, S. E. The Lively Experiment. Harper. $4.00.

Morgan, E. S. The Puritan Dilemma: The Story of John Winthrop. Little, Brown. $2.25.

Neusner, Jacob. American Judaism. Prentice Hall, $3.50.

Niebuhr, H. R. The Social Sources of Denominationalism. Meridian (World). $2.45.

Smith, H. S. et al. American Christianity. 2 vols. Scribner's. $9.95 ea.

Stedman, M. S., Jr. Religion and Politics in America. Harcourt, Brace and World. $2.95.

Stark, Rodney and Glock, Charles Y. American Piety: The Nature of Religious Commitment. University of California Press. $6.75.

Stokes, A. P. and Pfeffer, L. Church and State in the United States. Harper. $12.50.

Sweet, W. W. Religion in Colonial America. (Scribner's, 1942). Cooper. $6.95.

Tussman, Joseph (ed.) The Supreme Court on Church and State. Oxford University Press. $1.95.

Wilson, J. F. Church and State in American History. D. C. Heath. $2.50.

Yearbook of American Churches. National Council of Churches. (Annual Volume). $7.50.

CORRELATION OF RELIGIOUS ISSUES IN AMERICAN CULTURE

WITH LEADING SOCIAL STUDIES TEXTBOOKS

Textbooks

- A. Abramowitz, Jack. American History Study Lessons
- B. Bragdon, Henry W. and Samuel P. McCutchen. History of a Free People
- C. Dunwiddie, William E. and Horace Kidger. Problems of Democracy
- D. Eibling, Harold H., Fred M. King and James Harlow. History of Our United States
- E. Eibling, Harold H., Fred M. King, James Harlow and Milton Finkelstein. The Story of America
- F. Glanzrock, Jay. Adventures in American History
- G. Heller, Landis R. and Norris W. Potter. One Nation Indivisible
- H. McCutchen, Samuel P. and George L. Fersh. Goals of Democracy
- I. Madgic, Robert F., et al. The American Experience
- J. Schwartz, Melvin and John O'Conner. Exploring American History
- K. Shafer, Boyd C., Everett Augspurger and R. A. McLemore. United States History for High Schools
- L. Todd, Lewis Paul and Merle Curti. Rise of the American Nation
- M. Wilder, Howard B., Robert P. Ludlum and Harriett McCune Brown. This is America's Story

Textbooks	A	B	C	D,E	F	G	H	I	J	K	L	M
Study	Units	Chap.	Chap.	Chap.	Chap.	Chap.	Chap.	Chap.	Units	Chap.	Chap.	Chap.
1. Why Go to the New World?	1	1		3, 4	2, 3	1, 2		1	1	1	1, 5	3, 4
2. Conformity or Diversity?	1	1		4	4	2, 3	9	1	1, 2	1, 2	2, 5	4
3. The American Revolution: A Religious War?	1	2, 3		6	6	5		2	2	3	3, 5, 6	7, 8, 9
4. Subsidy or Separation?	2		20	8		6, 9	3		4	5, 8	12
5. The Churches on the American Frontier	3, 6	14, 19		12, 14, 15, 19	9, 14, 18	11	9, 13	7	4	10, 14	4, 16, 22	5, 16, 21
6. Blacks and the Churches	4, 9	11, 13, 15	9	12, 16	15, 26	13, 20, 31	7, 10	4, 5, 6	5 Concl.	11, 20, 28	15, 17	15, 17, 19, 26

Study	Textbooks	A Units	B Chap.	C Chap.	D,E Chap.	F Chap.	G Chap.	H Chap.	I Chap.	J Units	K Chap.	L Chap.	M Chap.
7. Religion: Personal and Social		4 6 9	13 20 24	13	21	20	10 19 21	21 22	8 9 10	6	17 18 19 20	17 25 26 29	14 23 26
8. Ways of Understanding: Science and Religion									14		20 23		
9. Conscience or Constitution?					30			9	14 19			9	
10. America: Protestant or Pluralist?		6 9	15 27	9	22	19	19 25	10 23 26	19 21	6	20 23	14 25	25 36

1

WHY GO TO THE NEW WORLD?

THE PLAN OF STUDY

Introduction

Sir Humphrey Gilbert, "A Discourse on How Her Majesty May Annoy the King of Spain." Reading with guiding questions.

Reverend Richard Hakluyt, "A Discourse on Western Planting" (1584). Reading with guiding questions.

Contemporary Parallel

Suggested Activities

Vocabulary

Resource Guide

THE FOCUS OF THIS STUDY

This study focuses upon the concept of motivation. A primary objective of social education is to bring students to know not only what happens in society but why it happens. In this case we want to find out why people undertake certain courses of action. Of course, one cannot hope to ascertain exactly why (to the exclusion of all other possibilities) an individual or group acts in a particular manner. But, students can learn that overt behavior does not immediately reveal the precise motive for such behavior. Also, students can understand that single motives seldom explain action. Rather, a complex of motives usually lies behind observable human undertakings.

Teachers and students will immediately see that they daily infer motives for behavior observed and that the systematic examination of such inferences is directly applicable to their lives as students and as adults. We "understand" why a person or group did something by referring to intentions, motives, thoughts, values, plans, attitudes, and desires. Consider just the court room where matters of motive are of vital concern in adjudicating a case! Consider these explanations: Napoleon was motivated by a will to power. Sam flew the flag because he is patriotic. Mary let Jack copy her home work because she has a crush on him. Cardinal Richelieu's policy was guided throughout his aim to establish a centralized French monarchy. Pope Urban II called for the First Crusade to protect pilgrims in the Holy Land.

Explanation in terms of motive is not an easy or a simple matter. Students might begin, however, by noting that human behavior is goal-directed. Men allocate their scarce resources to achieve goals which they value; generally, the greater they value a goal, the more they are "motivated" to achieve it (e.g., the more attention and resources they will allocate to achieve it). Psychologists who have examined personality and human motives, mostly concur that humans tend to value and are motivated to achieve goals in a sequence beginning with basic physiological needs for survival:[1]

      6. To know and understand
      5. Self-actualization
     4. Self-esteem needs
    3. Love and belonging needs
   2. Safety-security needs
1. Physiological needs

Such a diagram offers insights to explain human behavior. However, few persons would try to predict an actor's behavior based upon such a model. Similarly, the proposition, that behavior is goal-directed and values influence the allocation of scarce resources, is insightful but not predictive. George C. Homans in The Nature of Social Science[2] explored the answer to the question: Why did William the Conqueror never invade Scotland? Generally, the answer would be that he had no desire for the lands of the Scotish nobles, and thus, he merely fought to secure his borders from Malcolm, King of Scotland. But Homans offers this logical set of propositions:

> The greater the value of a reward to a person, the more likely he is to take action to get that reward.

> In the given circumstances, William the Conqueror did not find the conquest of Scotland worth the resources required.

> Thus, he was unlikely to take action that would win him Scotland.

Any question about the validity of this judgment concerning William's motives and his reasons, would have to be grounded with references to the factual evidence.

Nicholas Rescher in his Introduction to Value Theory[3] emphasizes the need for evidence, and the difficulty in being certain, when dealing with inferences and explanations by motives. In the case of Joe Jones the evidence can support a probable motive, or likely motive, for his action:

> Joe Jones joined the Peace Corps, which is dedicated to eradicating problems in underdeveloped nations.

> Throughout his life, Joe has been concerned with poverty, hunger, and illiteracy in the world (witness this evidence).

> Thus, we might conclude that he is likely to have joined the Peace Corps for his humanitarian motives.

Still, the pattern of Joe's concerns and behavior do not yield a certain conclusion on the question of why he joined the Peace Corps. They only yield a probable conclusion on motives; and it is essential for students to realize the difficulties in even getting probable conclusions which are reliable.

---

[1] Abraham H. Maslow, "A Theory of Motivation," The Psychological Review, Volume 30 (1943), 370–396.

[2] (New York: Harcourt, Brace & World, Inc., 1967), p. 44.

[3] (Englewood Cliffs, N.J.: Prentice-Hall, Inc., 1969), pp. 26–27.

Confronted with the question, Why did Brutus stab Caesar?, the student should learn to see that this is requesting an explanation in terms of <u>motive</u> (What did Brutus think, which made him decide to stab Caesar?). The student might first seek to find Brutus' goal with reference to the data on the historical instance. If the goal was the preservation of the Republic, the student may build his case: "Brutus joined the conspiracy against Caesar because of his devotion to the Republic. He believed that Caesar's political machinations would weaken or destroy the Republic, and he was convinced that the conspirators' plot was the last remaining effective means for impeding this development. Eager to preserve the Republic at virtually any cost, etc. . . ."[1] The student building such an explanation would have to rely upon any stated motives by the actor, his pattern of behavior and thought before and after the deed, and evidence from other than Brutus. Still the explanation is likely or probabilistic—not conclusive—and the student must remain skeptical. Inferring the motive from the deed, gathering evidence about what goes on in another man's mind, are not simple matters.

Patrick Gardiner in his <u>The Nature of Historical Explanation</u>[2] discusses the historian's use of explanation by motive:

> An historian tells us that Napoleon's actions were motivated by a will to power. What was this "will to power?" Was it like the force that drives a locomotive, a spiritual steam which made its appearance whenever he took a decision or drafted an order? Could its manifestations be observed, timed, predicted, reported upon? Did Napoleon feel them coming on? Did they stop before he lifted his pen or opened his mouth, or was he aware of them persisting simultaneously with his actions? Were they always present, whether he was engaged in activity or not, like a toothache? What happened when he was asleep? Could his urge to power be turned off when he grew tired of it?
>
> Questions like these are useful in making clear the boundaries within which it is safe to use the expression "he was motivated by a will to power." For example, when an historian uses it about Napoleon, his usage is considered in this case to be correct if he is able to <u>give instances</u> of Napoleon seizing opportunities that led to an increase in his prestige and authority, rejecting other courses of action which would have led to different results, working hard upon plans and projects for his personal advancement, showing irritation when he was frustrated, reporting perhaps in a diary, or in letters, or in memoirs, upon his aims, his feelings, or his moods. . . .
>
> "When in doubt as to why a person did something, put yourself in his position" may be a useful methodological precept, but it is far from always being reliable. People differ. From the fact that, if I did x, it would be because I wanted y (i.e. would have been satisfied if y occurred, would have given y as my aim if asked, &c.), it does not follow that when a medieval baron did x he wanted y. To find out whether y was really the reason for someone's doing x, we need more facts, not more intuition. . . .
>
> (1) Part of what we mean when we say that an emotion is "intentional" or "done for a purpose" may be that at some time or another a certain plan has been formulated by the agent to which the action conforms. (2) When we decide, in our own case, why we did something on a particular occasion we do not perform a mysterious act of "looking inside" for mental entities called "motives"—we may, on the other hand, do it by remembering how we formulated the matter to ourselves before we acted, but we may also do it by recalling the kind of reasons we should have given if someone had asked us what we were about either during or after the performance of the action in question, and we may again do it in some cases by ignoring the

---

[1] Ibid.
[2] (New York: Oxford University Press, 1961), pp. 121, 129–130, 134–135, 136.

ostensible reasons we gave to ourselves or to others and by considering instead other factors such as our reactions and feelings when a certain state of affairs was performed (perhaps its similarities with other occasions upon which we have acted in the past), and our knowledge of our own character and personality. (3) When we are called upon to decide why a person other than ourselves acted as he did, the criteria we use are always and necessarily what he does or what he tells us. The inference involved when we infer that someone else has such-and-such an aim or motive is inference to what on actual occasions he has done or said or to what on hypothetical occasions he would do or say. The demand that the criteria should be the same both in cases where we are deciding upon the nature of our own motives and in cases where we are deciding upon the nature of the motives of another person is an illegitimate one, and its origin must be attributed to the assimilation of talk about motives and actions to talk about causes and effects.

It may be objected that we make use of our own experience when we are assessing the motives of others. This must be, and has been, admitted. But to admit it is not to admit the proposition frequently alleged to follow from it, that our own experience is in some way transformed into the experience of the person whose motives we are examining, that when, for example an historian is said to understand why Caesar crossed the Rubicon he becomes Caesar and intuitively rethinks in his own mind thoughts which are literally identical with Caesar's thoughts on the occasion in question. We all know (it would be an abuse of language to say that we "assume") that people often act rationally, that in many situations they can be counted upon to give us good reasons for that which they are doing and to do it in a certain kind of way. As rational beings ourselves, accustomed to choose between various methods of attaining certain results, it is not surprising that we are able, readily and often without hesitation, to understand why, in similar situations, other people have acted as they have, and to imagine the sort of reasons they would have given for the actions they performed, had they been asked. That it should have been thought that there is a mystery about this is itself a mystery....

... By examining what we know of his other behaviour, of the time at which he lived, of the situation in which he was placed, perhaps by comparing what he did with what we should have done in like circumstances.[1] These represent the kind of criteria historians are in the habit of applying. More they cannot do. And the impossibility involved is not a causal or physical impossibility—there is no empirical barrier—but, as has been said, a logical one. The only state of affairs which would satisfy our objector would be one in which the historian actually was all the characters about whom he writes.

OBJECTIVES FOR THIS STUDY

<u>Knowledge Objectives</u>—Each student will demonstrate his knowledge that:

1. Motives lie behind the observable actions of individuals and groups.

2. Usually more than one motive is needed to explain a certain action.

3. A given course of action may be undertaken by different people for differing motives.

---

[1] "The real reasons" (e.g., for an action) is an expression almost as open to abuse as the expression "the real causes." Indeed, the two phrases are frequently referred to as if they were identical in meaning, a fact responsible for considerable confusion. In general, it appears safe to say that by a man's "real reasons" we mean those reasons he would be prepared to give under circumstances where his confession would not entail adverse consequences to himself. An exception to this is the psychoanalyst's usage of the expression where different criteria are adopted.

4. Motives behind historical events are often hidden and must be searched out, if possible.

5. England's colonization of America was the result of a complex of religious and secular motives.

Skill Objectives—Each student will demonstrate his ability to:

1. Analyze primary sources for styles of argumentation and information about human motives.

2. Extract explicit motives (reasons) for a course of action from historical documents.

3. Identify emotion-ladden words in an argument designed to persuade another to follow a certain course of action.

4. Hypothesize about motives for courses of action, grounding explanations by motives with the available evidence and realizing the tentative nature of inferences concerning motives.

Value and Attitude Objectives—Each student will demonstrate his willingness to:

1. Consider different points of view and weigh supporting arguments on a disputed issue in class discussion.

2. Be skeptical about inferring implicit motives from overt behavior and about statements attributing motives to an individual or group.

3. Suspend judgment until adequate information is known, and test beliefs and assumptions with evidence from specific historical and contemporary instances.

INTRODUCTION

To introduce students to the study of historical motivation, we look first at motives behind activities familiar to most teen-agers. The basic question is "What motives lie behind these activities?"

1. getting a summer or part-time job
2. inviting certain people to a party
3. reading a particular book from an English class list

The answers will reveal that individuals undertaking the same actions may do so for a variety of motives.

Students should first read the Introduction to the study, "Why Go to the New World?" Then, the class may be divided into four groups. Allow the groups fifteen minutes to develop a list of possible motives for the specific activity assigned to them. Class discussion can then proceed as each group lists motives on the blackboard.

In the discussion, ask students to support their suggestions. Ask how they might go about determining just why someone is acting as he is. Explore, also, the possibility of multiple motives. Can a student read a book for more than one reason? Might a teen-ager get a summer job for one reason while his parents encourage him for another? Do students have different motives for inviting various people to a party? Might I go to church for one reason and you for another?

The primary aims of this discussion are to have students know (1) that motives exist, (2) that determining motives helps to explain events and (3) that usually more than one motive is needed to explain any given action.

Further discussion might consider the evaluation of motives (i.e., "Are his motives honorable?"), determining also whether they are extrinsic (i.e., "I go to camp because my parents made me go") or intrinsic (i.e., "I read this book because it fascinates me").

England is Encouraged to Venture into the New World

England's colonization of North America is a familiar story. Junior and senior high school students have read the descriptions of exploits of John Smith, the Pilgrims and Puritans, and Lord Baltimore. Unfortunately, the motives of America's colonizers have too often been oversimplified. Typically, purely religious motives have been assigned to certain colonial ventures, while purely secular motives have been applied to others. Students have seldom been asked to examine critically the complex nature of human motivation itself.

In this study, two original sources are presented for student examination. Each reading offers different reasons for England's venturing into the New World. Shortly after these "Discourses" appeared, England did enter the competition for colonies. Why she did so cannot be fully determined in this brief study. What this study can provide is an opportunity to investigate the possible motives for English colonizing, to hypothesize about the strength of various motives, and to draw conclusions subject to repeated modification as more information becomes available.

The readings may be done at home or in class. Questions are provided to guide students through the readings.
If you need to help individual students with the guiding questions, the following should be considered.

SIR HUMPHREY GILBERT

1. What is Sir Humphrey Gilbert asking permission to do? Why does he say, "I will undertake this without your Majesty's being responsible"?

Essentially Sir Humphrey was asking to be supported in piracy. He wished to attack and destroy the shipping even of nations not at war with England. Sir Humphrey assured the Queen that her role would be kept secret. For England was then at peace with the nations in question—Spain, France, and Portugal. Open and official piracy would surely lead to war. So if Gilbert were captured or his deeds became known, Elizabeth would disclaim any part in his ventures.

2. What will be the primary gain for the English queen if Gilbert's plan is successful?

By Gilbert's piracy, England's enemies will be made weak and poor. At the same time, England will become stronger and richer at their expense.

3. What arguments against his plan has Gilbert foreseen and sought to answer? Are these good answers?

One argument against his plan is that Gilbert will destroy only the shipping of private interests, not the navies of France, Spain, and Portugal. Gilbert answers that the "princes" will suffer greatly from his destruction of even private vessels. For the princes' ships are small and few in number. They depend upon their subject's trade for their revenues. When these ships are destroyed, their owners will be ruined, their business lost. By these losses, the princes in turn lose their power.

Another argument is that the plan is not "allowable." It violates England's treaties and God's law. Sir Humphrey answers, "I hold it as lawful in Christian policy to prevent a mischief in time as to revenge it too late." He notes further that God himself is a party to England's quarrels with the (Roman Catholic) nations of Spain, France, and Portugal. Gilbert avers that God will support Elizabeth in this undertaking.

In guiding class discussion, the teacher also might use the following set of questions which emphasize the problem of justifying policy decisions and recommendations:

1. What is proposed as a course of action?

2. What consequences can be expected? Is this projection of consequences valid (reasonable, supported by what is known)?

3. Are the consequences desirable? Are these consequences better than the consequences of the alternative courses of action open? Here the criteria for judging consequences concern values and the goals sought. How does Gilbert perceive the values of the queen as implied in his argument on the desirability of the consequences)? What are the values he uses to assert the desirability of consequences?

Questions under the map:

Why might Sir Humphrey suggest Newfoundland for his operations? Why might Denmark and Holland be good places to take captured ships?

Use the map to show the distance between Newfoundland and England. Newfoundland is closer than other New World land to England. Also commercial fishing activity off the Newfoundland coast was highly profitable.

Denmark and Holland were friendly nations. Gilbert could expect aid from them since they had a common enemy in the Catholic power. They also had large and safe harbors, near to England's coast.

RICHARD HAKLUYT

1. What part of the New World is Hakluyt talking about? Find "30 degrees in Florida northward unto 63 degrees."

Use the map to find the North American places referred to by Hakluyt. Point out the extent and grandeur of Hakluyt's envisioned mission: from Florida to Hudson Bay. Note how this does coincide with the area of subsequent English colonization.

2. What plan does Hakluyt have for avoiding the fate of the first Spanish missionaries in Florida? Does this make sense?

Hakluyt advises that colonists be sent to live in the New World. The colonists should first learn the language and customs of the natives. Presumably, the colonists can also win their friendship and confidence. Additionally, the settlers' numerical strength will provide safety and support. Gradually, then the colonists may acquaint the natives with Christianity.

This is far better, says Hakluyt, than the rash attempts of the Spanish friars. More than once Spain had sent missionaries into a hostile and utterly unknown territory, with the result being a savage and sudden slaughter of the foreign intruders.

3. What is "filthy lucre and vain ostentation"? Why might Hakluyt refer to this here?

"Filthy lucre" is, literally, dirty money. Many European nations were drawn to the New World by the promise of riches. Furthermore, they displayed "vain ostentation," that is, an indulgence in the trappings of national power and splendor. Hakluyt was probably thinking of Spain which had derived great wealth from exploiting the New World. The gold brought back by Spanish fleets raised the prestige of Spain throughout Europe.

4. What chain of reasoning does Hakluyt use to support his argument that the English monarch should send preachers to the New World?

The natives of the New World are in immortal danger. They cannot call on the Lord to be saved because "they have not heard." The Apostle Paul wrote that preachers must be sent to those who have not heard the gospel. These preachers, says Hakluyt, should be sent by those who are protectors and defenders of the Christian faith. The Kings and Queens of England have the title "Defender of the faith." Thus, "they are charged not only to maintain and favor the faith of Christ, but also to enlarge and advance it." From Hakluyt's point of view, moreover, the English monarchs are defenders of the "True and sincere religion"—that is, Protestantism.

After students have read Gilbert and Hakluyt, class discussion should be directed toward helping students answer the central question, "Why go to the New World?" Emphasis is not on arriving at an agreed answer, but on the process of reaching probable answers. In this process students must evaluate the information gained from the readings. They must analyze parts of the writings, see relationships among them, determine what is significant. They must synthesize their information. Do the readings have points in common? Do these give us clues to the real motives for English colonization? Students should develop their own hypotheses about the motives for settlement. These must be subjected to evaluation. Finally, based on the information provided, what tentative conclusion about England's motives can we reach.

CLASS DISCUSSION

When you lead the class discussion, the following should be considered.

1. Gilbert and Hakluyt each urged Queen Elizabeth to venture into the New World. Yet, the advice of each is quite different.

   a. On what points might they agree? Why?

Gilbert and Hakluyt would probably agree that England's venture into the new world would (and should) benefit the Church of England. They might also agree that England would be strengthened in her rivalry with foreign powers. However, the "filthy lucre and vain ostentation" which Hakluyt condemned were probably prime movers of Sir Humphrey. Also, we might not expect Hakluyt to go along with either Gilbert's plan or his justifications for it. Conversely, it is doubtful Sir Humphrey would agree that the saving of souls should be the primary gain of England's colonial efforts.

b. On what points would you expect them to disagree? Why would you expect them to disagree on some points?

We should expect the two men to differ in as much as the <u>one was a clergyman, the other an adventurer</u>.

2. Motives play an important role in determining courses of action.

   a. Give a name to the major motives of Sir Humphrey Gilbert.

   b. Give a name to the major motives of Richard Hakluyt.

   A number of names could be given to characterize the major motives of each man. Students should offer their own suggestions. You might list these suggestions on the blackboard and discuss the suitability of each term or name.

   c. Could an individual hold the motives of both? Why? Why not?

   An individual living in Elizabethan England might very well share the motives held both by Gilbert and Hakluyt. He might also argue against any contradiction existing between them. It should be pointed out that in sixteenth century <u>Europe nations fought under religious banners, temporal rulers claimed divine sanction for their acts, and churches enjoyed government power. The fortunes of church and state were closely bound</u>.

3. In the writings of both Gilbert and Hakluyt, <u>God is mentioned.</u>

   a. <u>What role does Gilbert imply God will take in the New World venture?</u>

   Gilbert implies that God will aid England in this venture. First, he notes "God has especially provided for your majesty's safety." Later, he adds "that God Himself is a party to the common quarrels (with Catholic nations) now afoot." The enemies' evil disposition toward the Queen and the Church of England has not had effect because of "God's merciful providence."

   b. Would Hakluyt agree with him? Why? Why not?

   Hakluyt could be expected, as a clergyman, to discern the hand of God in human actions. He might agree with Gilbert that God protects England and the Church of England. Hakluyt certainly assumes that God would play a positive role in the plan for spreading Christianity to the New World. This is "fruitful labor in God's harvest." God will move the heart of Queen Elizabeth "to put her helping hand to this godly action." Yet, Hakluyt and Gilbert might well differ on the kind of action thought to be "godly action."

4. The readings refer to England's relations with other nations.

   a. What was the nature of England's relations with Spain at this time?

   b. Why might the New World be a vital factor in this relationship?

   c. Was religion an important aspect of English-Spanish relations? Why? Why not?

   <u>England, had, under Henry VIII, established its own national church, the Church of England, and renounced the authority of the Pope. This placed England in opposition to Catholic powers</u>

in Europe of whom Spain was the most powerful. During the long reign of Elizabeth (1558–1603) relations with Spain remained severely strained. Religion was not the only cause of English-Spanish conflict. Spain's exploration and exploitation of the New World brought her money and prestige. Englishmen and Spaniards vied for commercial and naval supremacy, the contest being waged on the high seas from the coasts of Western Europe to the West Indies. Daring English 'sea-dogs' plundered Spanish galleons loaded with gold, raided Spanish ports, and brought frustration to the throne. The most spectacular event of the protracted and sporadic hostilities was the destruction of the Spanish Armada in 1588. This pivotal event opened the way for England's entry into the New World in a permanent and powerful fashion.

5. England did, of course, enter the New World as a colonial power. Sir Walter Raleigh planted the ill-fated Roanoke Colony in 1587, only ten years after Gilbert wrote his "Discourse." Later, settlers came to Jamestown in 1607 and Plymouth in 1620.

a. Would settlers in these colonies have similar motives for coming to America as the monarch who sent them? Why? Why not?

Colonists and colonizing monarchs seldom had the same motives for their actions. Religion and economics may have moved monarchs as it did settlers, but in vastly different ways. The economic rivalry among European nations stimulated exploration and colonization. Colonies could bring economic advantage; thus, monarchs supported colonies. Settlers came because of economic motives, too, but they sought private gain more than national advantage. The hardships experienced by the Englishman in "making ends meet" often spurred him to the New World. The lure of great wealth often drew those of higher station to become colonial "adventurers." The religious hostility between Protestant and Catholic powers influenced some monarchs in their support of missionary efforts. In other instances the zeal to enlarge Christendom may have been equally strong. The religious motives of colonists could range from preaching to the Indians to seeking an escape from all "public religion" to a private freedom of conscience.

b. Is Sir Walter Raleigh's list of motives (in the introduction) complete? Could you add more?

As we have seen, many motives can lie behind a single action. Men came to the New World to be free to worship as they chose (for "religion"), to find gold (for "wealth"), because they were curious (for "knowledge"), because they loved adventure (for "pleasure"), or in the hope of finding a Northwest Passage, winning "power" and bringing about the "overthrow of rivals." But students may wish to add to Raleigh's list, offering examples and evidences of their own.

c. Do you feel that England's entry into the New World was the result of a single overriding motive? Or, do you believe it was the result of a complex of motives? Explain.

National motives are even more complex than personal ones. To explain England's actions, one may now look to religion, next to politics, later to economics. One may find these, and others, so mixed together as to make the determination of a "major motive" impossible.

CONTEMPORARY PARALLEL

President John Kennedy addressed the United States Congress on May 25, 1961: "Now it is time to take longer strides, time for a great new American enterprise, time for this nation to take a clearly leading role in space achievement, which in many ways may hold the key to our future on earth." Forty seconds after 4:17 A.M. EST, July 20, 1969, man had landed on the moon. In an historic telephone call from the planet earth to the planet moon—a quarter of a million miles away—President Richard Nixon praised the feat of the astronauts: "Because of what you have done, the heavens have become a part of man's world, and as you talk to us from the Sea of Tranquillity, it inspires us to bring peace and tranquillity to earth."

"Why Go to the Moon?" offers a contemporary parallel to the issues raised in this study, "Why Go to the New World?" What were the motives behind this twenty-four billion dollar effort? Do the statements by Kennedy and Nixon reveal the motives? How about Neil Armstrong's words, "One small step for man, one giant leap for mankind?" Or the words on the plaque, "They came in peace for all mankind"? Were the motives geared more to the political realities of the cold war, i.e., "beating Russia to the moon"? What about motives involving a spy system of satellites or communication via satellites? Was the motive to explore outer space simply "because it's there"? Buzz Aldrin spoke these words from space on the voyage home: "We've come to the conclusion that this has been far more than three men on a voyage to the moon, or still, than the efforts of a government and industry team, or even than the efforts of one nation. We feel that this stands as a symbol of the insatiable curiosity of all mankind to explore the unknown." What does this suggest about motivation?

"Why go to Vietnam?" Perhaps this question offers the most obvious parallel to the issues raised in the study, "Why Go to the New World?" Secretary of State Dulles made the first official statement of our country's motivation on July 24, 1954, shortly after the French were forced to withdraw from North Vietnam. Dulles declared that U.S. policy was "not to mourn the past but to seize future opportunities to prevent the loss in North Vietnam from leading to the extension of Communism throughout Southeast Asia and the Southwest Pacific." Other motives expressed by spokesmen for U.S. involvement have included the containment of China, preserving the freedom of the South Vietnamese, protecting South Vietnam from "aggression from the north," defending American honor, and the like. Critics of the United States' role have challenged these as the "real" motives, suggesting that the major motive is to "use" the Saigon regime as an anti-communist base in the pursuit of cold war objectives in relation to China and the U.S.S.R. Students can find references to motives in newspapers, radio and television reports, speeches, and articles. Folk songs and rock music abound in references to our motives for being in Vietnam. Two of the most biting commentaries are Pete Seeger's "Talking Ben Tre" and Country Joe McDonald's "I Feel Like I'm Fixin' to Die Rag."

Bob Dylan's "With God on Our Side" is an appropriate contemporary response to the claim that both Gilbert and Hakluyt make for "God's merciful providence" in behalf of England. Dylan's song recites the killing by people with God on their side in the Spanish-American War, the First World War, the Second World War, and now the cold war.

Another area of the world where the motives of the United States government are much discussed is Latin America. Students could list motives for the various U.S. aid programs and attempt to evaluate them: the Military Assistance Program, the Alliance for Progress, the Foreign Assistance Act, the U.S. Agency for International Development, and the Overseas Education Fund.

Other current issues related to the emphases of this study could deal with such questions as the following: What are the motives of the American youth who emigrate from the United States to Canada? Why do young people join the Peace Corps or Vista ACTION? What motivates the modern-day missionaries? What are the motives behind our space program?

Students might also be intrigued with the idea that migration does not have to be physical. What about the motives of those persons who are pioneers in exploring the frontiers of knowledge and human relations?

As students delve into the realm of motivation, they will come to see the difficulty in distinguishing between motives that are "religious" and those that are "secular." Ethicists remind us that every moral decision involves the four factors of the ends, the means, the motives, and the foreseeable consequences. However, they are reluctant to ascribe love as a unique motive to religious people. Some Christian moralists have suggested that the only uniqueness of the Christian love ethic is in the nature of its motivation as a responsive love, a loving response to God's love in Christ. But these are subtle and complex distinctions. If we can impress students with the difficulty of making judgments in respect to motives—their own, other individuals, groups and nations—this study will have made an important contribution to their understanding.

SUGGESTED ACTIVITIES

Written Assignment—"Memo to the Queen"

As an official in the English government, you are asked to evaluate the comments of Gilbert and Hakluyt and to prepare a brief memorandum for the Queen's advisers. In the memo list the arguments stated by Gilbert and Hakluyt, offering your reaction to each. Also, list other points—for and against going to the New World—which you feel the advisers should consider.

Here the emphasis is upon critical evaluation of the arguments offered by Gilbert and Hakluyt—looking at them from the point of view of national interest. Adding arguments not offered by either man offers students an excellent exercise in historical imagination.

Suggestions for Further Research

These areas of investigation are suggested for those students wishing to do additional research. In guiding students in their individual efforts, be sure to use the "Basic Library" as well as the Resource Guide below.

1. Richard Hakluyt was very concerned with "bringing the gospel to idolators." How successful were the attempts to convert the American Indians? Hakluyt was also concerned lest the Roman Catholic Church enjoy the only success in bringing Christianity to the Indians. Did this church continue to have a "monopoly" in mission effort among the Indians?

2. Various motives have been assigned to the settlers of the English colonies. What were the major motives in the settling of (a) Maryland, (b) Massachusetts, (c) New York? Are multiple motives to be found in each colony?

VOCABULARY

abridged
adversary
contentious
discourse
enterprise
impoverish
ladings

license
lucre
manifest
motivation
ostentation
realm
traffic

RESOURCE GUIDE FOR STUDY 1

I. Audio Visual Aids

A. Films

Age of Discovery. 15 min., b&w, rental $3.50
   McGraw-Hill Films, 330 W. 42nd St., New York, N.Y. 10009
This film summarizes and assesses the factors that motivated men to discover and explore the New World. It could serve as a culminating activity.

French Explorations in the New World. 11 min., b&w, rental $2.25.
   Coronet Films, 65 E. South Water St., Chicago, Illinois, 60601
Tracing the pattern of exploration through Verrazano, Cartier, Champlain, Marquette, Joliet, and La Salle, shows how soldier-explorers and missionaries planted the earliest settlements and laid the foundation for French strongholds in the New World.

Historic Plymouth. 14 min., color, rental $5.25
   International Film Bureau, 332 South Muligan Ave., Chicago, Illinois 60604
This film shows what still remains of the first colony in America at Plymouth Rock. Scenes visually support the place where the Pilgrims encountered Indians, constructed the first buildings. The annual reenactment by the people of Plymouth of "Pilgrim's Progress" is also pictured.

Pilgrim Adventure. 54 min., color, rental $17.50
   McGraw-Hill Films, 330 W. 42nd St., New York, N.Y. 10009
Traces the pilgrims' flight from England to Holland and then to the New World. Shows religious motivation and hardships endured in New England.

The Pilgrims. 22 min., b&w, rental $4.50
   Encyclopedia Britannica Films, 425 N. Michigan Ave., Chicago, Illinois 60611
The Pilgrims' religious persecution in England, poverty in Holland, terrible North Atlantic crossing, signing of the Mayflower Compact, heroic efforts to survive the bitter New England winter, and the first Thanksgiving are among the highlights that are brought alive in this film by the authentic set and period costumes.

Plymouth Colony: The First Year. 16 min., color, rental $5.40
   Coronet Films, 64 E. South Water St., Chicago, Illinois 60601
Scenes filmed at authentically reconstructed "Plymouth Plantation" at Plymouth, Mass., and on the Mayflower II. This film tells of the great struggle with hardship, disease, and the fight for freedom and democracy.

Roger Williams: Founder of Rhode Island. 28 min., b&w, rental $8.00
   Encyclopedia Britannica Films, 425 N. Michigan Ave., Chicago, Illinois 60611
Re-creates the dramatic story of Roger Williams' conflict with the Puritan leaders of New England; his fight for separation of church and state, freedom of conscience, and protection for minority groups; the "heresy" trial which resulted in his banishment from the Massachusetts Bay Colony; and his decision to establish a new colony.

Sir Francis Drake (The Rise of English Sea Power). 14 min., b&w, rental $3.65
   Encyclopedia Britannica Films, 425 N. Michigan Ave., Chicago, Illinois 60611
With rich authentic settings and superb English cast, the film re-creates the most important episodes in Drake's life—shows how he won England the right of way into a new continent;

captured a vast treasure of gold, silver and precious stones for his Queen; terrorized the Spanish navy, and persuaded the people of England to find their strength in the sea. This film could be used to provide a background for the "Discourses" of Sir Humphrey Gilbert and Richard Hakluyt.

Spanish Influences in the United States. 10 min., b&w, rental $2.25
 Coronet Films, 65 E. South Water St., Chicago, Illinois 60601
Tells of importance of Spanish heritage visible in architecture, furniture, music, and language. Looking at the country, the children in this film discover the Spanish missions from Florida to California, the horses and cattle originally brought by the Spanish, and many other things.

The Trapdoor. 30 min. Eternal Light (kinescope)
 $8.50
How Jewish settlers in Newport, R. I. came to understand the American principle of religious freedom.

B. Filmstrips

 Apostle to the Indians. 15 min., color, sale $6.50
  American Bible Society, 1963, 1865 Broadway, New York, New York 11023
 This film tells the story of the Puritan preacher, John Eliot, and his work with the North American Indians. He learned the language of the Indians, translated the Bible into it, taught them to read and write, and helped improve living conditions.

 The Jews Settle in New Amsterdam–1654. 37 frames. $9.50. Union of American Hebrew
  Congregations, 838 Fifth Avenue, New York, N. Y. 10021
 How the first Jews came to the American colonies in search of religious freedom.

II. Articles

"Digging Up Jamestown," American Heritage, vol. 14 (April, 1963).

"Far Cry," Saturday Review, vol. 50 (December 30, 1967).

"One Small Candle," Reader's Digest, vol. 83 (December, 1963).

"Our Puritan Roots," Nation, vol. 204 (May 29, 1967).

"Ultimate Courage of Jean de Brefeuf," American Heritage, vol. 10 (October, 1959).

III. Books

Acheson, Patricia C. America's Colonial Heritage. New York: Dodd, Mead. $3.75

Blau, Joseph L. The Spiritual Life of American Jewry, 1654–1954. (In American Jewish Year Book, Vol. 56, 1955. New York: American Jewish Committee. pp. 99–170)

Bolton, Ivy. Father Junipero Serra. New York: Messner. $3.50

Bradford, William. Of Plymouth Plantation: The Pilgrims in America. Putnam (Capricorn) (paper) $1.85

Ellis, John T. Catholics in Colonial America. New York: Helican Press. $10.00

Gaer, Joseph, and Ben Siegel. The Puritan Heritage: America's Roots in the Bible. New York: New American Library. (paper) $.75

Gannon, Michael V. The Cross in the Sand. University of Florida Press. (paper) $2.00

Kenton, Edna (editor) Jesuit Relations and Allied Documents, Travels and Explorations of the Jesuit Missionaries in North America (1610–1791). New York: Vanguard Press. $10.00

A Kino Guide: A Life of Eusebio Francisco Kino, Arizona's First Pioneer, and a Guide to his Missions and Monuments. Southwestern Mission Research Center (949 East 2nd St., Tucson, Arizona, 85791). (bound) $2.00

LaMonte, Enid Meadowcroft. The First Year. New York: T. Y. Crowell. $3.50 The story of the Pilgrims in America.

Wertenbaker, Thomas J. The Puritan Oligarchy. New York: Scribner. (paper) $2.95

Winslow, Ola E. John Eliot: Apostle to the Indians. Boston: Houghton Mifflin, $5.95

Wise, Winifred E. Fray Junipero Serra and the California Conquest. New York: Charles Scribner's Sons. $3.95

In the Basic Library particular attention is called to the following volumes:

Ellis, Documents of American Catholic History, Parts I, II, III

Gaustad, A Religious History of America, Parts I, II

Morgan, The Puritan Dilemma

2
CONFORMITY OR DIVERSITY?

THE PLAN OF THE STUDY

Introduction

William Penn, "The Great Case of Liberty of Conscience"

Thomas Barton, "A Letter to the Society for Propagation of the Gospel"

Contemporary Parallel

Suggested Activities

Vocabulary

Resource Guide

THE FOCUS OF THIS STUDY

The focus of this study is the issues surrounding the conflicts between demands for diversity and conformity, and unity and pluralism, in human groups and in entire societies. These issues are timeless, and men in all ages have sought answers to questions such as: How much conformity is essential to the survival of the society? To attain the goals of the organization? How much conformity is desirable? In the "good society" to what should "good men" conform? Basic values? Folkways? Certain kinds of behavior as spelled out in specific legislation? Or as demanded by informal social expectations? Questions concerning conformity raise correlary questions about freedom, its essence and desirability, especially as freedom produces a diverse society or group. As different societies and groups have wrought answers to these questions, how did they justify their answers? By expediency? By claims of undesirable consequences or desirable consequences? By received wisdom? By religious-philosophical systems?

In American history these questions arise time and again, beginning with the settlement around Massachusetts Bay, and these questions very often centered on religious matters. Demands for religious conformity have been heard across the land. The legal questions about the establishment of religion, religious toleration, and religious freedom have been argued throughout that history and continue in our own time. Public disputants have most often grounded their positions on these questions in terms of their conceptions of the "good society." The issue of conformity or diversity as a religious issue may be studied with reference to many periods of American history, but this Study draws upon the early history of Pennsylvania for a study of the issue. In the "Contemporary Parallel" section teachers may guide their students through discussions on the contemporary public issues, employing the skills and extending the value principles developed by studying the historic case. Each day's newspaper reminds us that the issue is contemporary, and that American commitments to pluralism are evolutionary.

The two historic documents employed in this Study and the issues raised permit students to learn several useful skills and to practice skills already attained. Students learn the difference between primary (underived, eyewitness, first-hand) and secondary sources which historians, and citizens, use in their daily search for reliable knowledge. They learn the rudimentary skills of internal criticism (the analysis of contents) and of the evaluation of the resulting data as evidence in making judgments. The two documents, the first by William Penn and the second from the hand of the Reverend Thomas Barton, are excellent for these learning tasks as Penn provides an explanation and argument based upon his plans, intentions, and motives, while Barton argues with a specific value commitment and evidence derived from his personal observations. Thus, students read two lively documents that display the role of frame of reference in argumentation and decision-making.

OBJECTIVES FOR THIS STUDY

Knowledge Objectives—Each student will demonstrate his knowledge that:

1. There have been serious conflicts over various views of society involving perceptions of the need for conformity and diversity, and that certain measures of conformity and diversity are needed for social stability and progress.

2. Religious conformity may be tied to the establishment of religion by social, and moral-ethical grounds.

3. Freedom of conscience may be defended on religious, political-social, and moral-ethical grounds.

4. Penn's colony was an experiment in allowing freedom of conscience.

5. The effect of freedom of conscience has promoted the religious diversity in America.

6. The issue of conformity and diversity in America has increasingly been resolved with commitment to the ideal that pluralism, based upon rational concent and promoting the dignity and worth of the individual personality, is the basis for a just society.

Skill Objectives—Each student will demonstrate his ability to:

1. Recognize manifestations of conformity and diversity in his daily surroundings.

2. Distinguish between primary and secondary sources.

3. Evaluate conclusions reached by an informant in terms of the warranting reasons and or evidence and his credibility as an informant.

4. Judge whether an observation statement by an informant is reliable, employing some of the analytical questions related to the historian's technique of internal criticism.

5. Generalize about the probable effect of conformity and diversity on society and religion.

Value and Attitude Objectives—Each student will demonstrate his willingness to:

1. Consider his own feelings and attitudes on specific instances involving the conformity-diversity issue, especially contemporary cases.

2. Question conclusions offered and their supporting arguments in the historical case and in contemporary, controversial cases.

3. Develop his value commitments on the conformity-diversity issue in contemporary America, especially in relation to the value of pluralism as a route to the "good society" and the meaning of justice within his society.

INTRODUCTION

The Attitude Scale

To introduce the Study a short attitude survey is used. The survey is designed to orient students to the central issue and to motivate thought. It begins close to home with statements obviously relevant to youth. Also, the first few statements concern practices, while the latter ones concern belief and may not be readily recognized as relevant by students.

(Since this scale is for motivational and class discussion purposes only, no attempt has been made to validate it. Thus, no attempt should be made to collect data from the survey, nor should student responses be compared or categorized as correct or incorrect answers.)

In discussion of the survey following administration, emphasis should be placed on suggesting reasons for either agreement or disagreement with each item. It is suggested that as many reasons as feasible be listed on the blackboard. From the discussion students should have been made aware of the dilemma-like nature and complexity of the issue of conformity vs. diversity. For Americans there are no easy answers. In an authoritarian society the issue is quickly settled by consulting tradition or ideology. In a society of many traditions and no official ideology, we must resolve such a conflict through an often lengthy democratic process.

For each item in the survey there is, of course, a conforming and a nonconforming attitude. A conforming attitude is indicated for each item by the following:

1. disagreement
2. agreement
3. agreement
4. agreement
5. agreement

It must be emphasized, however, that there is no right or wrong attitude. Neither conformity nor nonconformity per se is good or bad.

Understanding the Terms

An introduction to the concepts of conformity and diversity is presented in the student text. Additional background information on religious conformity follows in this manual. You may wish to include it in later discussions.

From conformity in general we now move to conformity that is specifically religious. Religious conformity has been, and still is, demanded in societies the world over. Problems of nonconformity have plagued nations for many centuries. Nonconformity has been seen, as it is by many today, as a threat to social stability and the established order. As such, its elimination has been vigorously pursued. The Western heritage reveals an ever-present struggle of conforming and nonconforming elements. Early Christian martyrs, Medieval heresies and the Huguenots in France may be seen as examples of diverse thinking or nonconformist actions. Indeed, in 16th century England, some Protestants were even officially labeled "Nonconformists."

The Renaissance, the Reformation and the Enlightenment opened the floodgates of opposition to established (i.e., conforming) religious persuasions. Increasingly, men challenged long accepted doctrines and time-honored institutions.

Unlike contemporary America, 18th century England accepted the church as an agency of government. To the church was entrusted the molding of minds. In the minds of believers the interests of God, church and government were wedded. The force of religious conviction could be relied upon to bring acquiescence to governmental will. Furthermore, bishops of the established church enjoyed peerage (membership in the House of Lords) and a measure of civil authority. In return for the social stability and domestic tranquillity fostered by the church, the government did its best to insure predominance, if not exclusiveness, of the established church in matters of faith.

While religious conformity was defended on social and political grounds, religious doctrine could also support establishment. Many devout Christian thinkers were convinced of the "correctness" of active government support of what they felt to be the true faith.

In the 17th and 18th centuries, diversity in thought and deed was viewed with much greater horror than today. The very foundations of the social and religious order would collapse if nonconforming views were allowed. Since that time, intellectual and political revolutions have taught that a measure of diversity is not only allowable but necessary. The degree of diversity permissable is, however, still much at issue.

Just as conformists supported their positions on various grounds, so do nonconformist thinkers. Diversity is argued on religious (as in Penn's case) as well as on political and social bases. Then, as today, certain grounds were more important to some than to others. Thus the nonbeliever may support diversity for one reason while the believer is impressed by another argument.

William Penn's colony in America provided us with one of the original experiments in full-scale religious freedom. While other American colonies were seeking orthodoxy, Pennsylvania afforded all who came there the freedom to pursue whatever religious persuasion they wished. In fact, Penn's own group, the Quakers, soon lost their ascendancy in Pennsylvania as the attraction of religious liberty rapidly filled the colony with a variety of faiths.

WILLIAM PENN

To gain knowledge of the "theory" behind the Pennsylvania experiment, students are presented with a portion of Penn's own case for freedom of conscience. His case is set forth on religious grounds. This approach is not as familiar to most students as the political-social or moral-ethical ones. Students should be aware that while such a basis might carry little weight for nonbelievers today, it was more important than "human" reasons for Penn and Christian thinkers of the past and present. Penn was able to implement his theory with the establishment of his colony in America. For an account of the results of freedom of conscience, we turn to an obviously hostile observer.

1. For Penn, religious liberty means not only a freedom to believe a certain way, but also a freedom to do what?

Penn is very much concerned with freedom in the practice of religion as well as belief. This practice, says Penn, is required by God.

2. In similar fashion, what does Penn mean by "persecution"?

Again, Penn is concerned with prohibitions against <u>practice</u> as well as <u>belief</u>. One persecutes when he interferes in any way with the practice of what God requires.

3. According to Penn, in what ways are rulers trying to assume the powers and rights of God?

Penn says that rulers usurp the powers and rights of God by:

    a. interfering with man's own rational judgment—a gift from God Himself
    b. claiming a god-like infallibility
    c. setting themselves up as rulers both of body and of soul
    d. forcing faith, which by its very nature is a gift of God, not the result of an act of coercion
    e. being accountable to none but themselves—leaving nothing to God

These questions ask students to identify the central issue, to specify definitions for terms as used, to recognize underlying and explicit assumptions, to analyze a logical, deductive argument, and to see the position of an informant's values and commitments in his decisions and judgments.

THOMAS BARTON

<u>Thomas Barton, it must be made clear, is a representative of the established order.</u> For him, conformity to that order is the best way to meet obligations to God, to his church, and to society at large. Barton views Penn's experiment with horror. He does not, though, speak against diversity on theological grounds.<u> He notes chaos and disharmony in the social order.</u> He sees his beloved Anglican Church consigned to a position of inferiority (in prestige) in this English colony.

1. What does Barton indicate has been the result of religious diversity? What assumptions does he make? What evidence does he use to support his judgment?

Barton notes that strife between groups is "tearing the province to pieces." Religious groups are hostile to each other. People are being led astray by strange doctrines.

2. What specifically does Barton suggest the government do to bring some Pennsylvanians into the church?

Barton believes that the German colonists might be brought into the church through a law requiring them to give their children an English education. He later suggests that Anglican bishops be established in the colony.

3. What kind of citizen does Barton think is best?

Barton's ideal citizen is peaceful and dutiful, submissive and obedient to civil authority.

4. What kind of observer do you consider Barton to be? A disinterested historian? An interested participant? A biased or a neutral reporter?

Barton is making 1) factual judgments about events and behavior which are caused by Pennsylvania's "religious diversity" and 2) policy recommendations based upon his perception of a problem, its cause, and the proper way to intervene to affect what he feels is the "good society."

In question 4 students are asked to assess Barton's credibility as an informant and his frame of reference and value commitments which guided his perception of a problem and his suggestion of policy. While answering the question, students should learn the kinds of analytical questions historians use to assess the creditability of an informant—questions which are useful to the student as citizen. Several of these questions are listed below:

Questions to ask an informant:

1. What are the informant's value commitments and his frame of reference?
2. What is the informant's position?
3. What reasons and evidence does the informant use to support his position? Do conclusions follow from the reasons and the evidence (Is the position warranted?)?
4. Where and how did the informant obtain his evidence? Was he an observer? Or did he rely on secondary sources?
   a. Was he able to tell the truth? In a position to know the truth? Was he an accurate observer?
   b. Was the informant willing to tell the truth? Was he a disinterested witness? A potential beneficiary?
   c. Can the informant's evidence be verified by independent witnesses (other informants)?

A DISCUSSION OF PENN AND BARTON

1. Both Penn and Barton seem sincerely concerned with the well-being of man, country and the Christian religion. Yet, they assume positions sharply opposed in achieving this well-being. Which of the two positions, Penn's or Barton's, do you believe would better promote:

   a. the growth and prosperity of a colony
   b. the well-being of a religious group

   a. Religion is, of course, only one factor related to the growth of a colony. However, if all those who did not conform in religion were excluded, there is the good chance that the special genius of many men would be lost to the colony. Immigrants of a variety of persuasions made great contributions to America. Also, a generally repressive and traditionalist atmosphere may be hostile to new ideas, thus thwarting progress. When men are free to follow their own conscience and to seek truth, society usually benefits. Societies strongly conformist in nature change little as new and diverse elements are stifled.

   b. While a religious group may enjoy a measure of material well-being due to the protection of secular institutions, the spiritual vitality may suffer. A group forced to stand on its own feet must develop inner resources. Also, dependence upon the state may obligate a group to that state, thus denying it the independence of thought and action needed to develop its theology.

2. William Penn defends freedom of conscience on religious grounds.

   a. For what type person would this argument have great appeal? To whom would it have little appeal?

   This argument would have great appeal to a religiously committed person. Particularly attracted would be those concerned with man's obligations to God. There would be little appeal to the nonbeliever, though he might support freedom of conscience on rational or humanistic grounds.

b. What other grounds might be used to defend freedom of conscience? What does Barton emphasize in opposing such freedom?

<u>Freedom of conscience may be argued in terms of ethical humanism, material progress, or political and social philosophy.</u> So <u>opposition to such freedom may be based on many grounds.</u> <u>Barton emphasizes deterioration of the social order and the attraction of strange novel doctrines in his opposition to freedom of religious belief and practice.</u>

3. Penn was very concerned with freedom in the practice of religion. Is freedom in practice necessary for freedom of belief (conscience)? If so, why? Why not?

Penn feels that men must be free to follow their conscience in matters of worship as well as belief. God, as He directs conscience, indicates the way in which He is to be worshipped. Men have no right to interfere with those trying to meet their obligations to God. Practice may be seen as the expression of obedience and belief. As such, it is a necessary element of freedom of conscience.

4. Should the government of England have been so concerned with the religious beliefs and practices of English subjects?

a. Give the reasons why government might involve itself in religious matters in the 17th and 18th centuries.

The English government had a quid pro quo (this for that) relationship with the Anglican Church. <u>While the government looked after the church, the church supported government policy and performed an educational function in gaining popular support for government.</u> Since the days of the Roman Emperor Constantine, government and church had worked together. Temporal rulers acted as God's agents on earth. <u>They played a role in church government and appointed bishops. Conversely, their rule was sanctioned by the church and their authority was long considered a gift of God</u> (Divine Right of Kings). With the Enlightenment, however, a gradual separation of ecclesiastical and political authority began. During the 17th and 18th centuries in England, traditional bonds between church and state remained strong though challenged by the nonconformists.

b. Does the U.S. government today ever concern itself with religion? How are its concerns different from those in England?

<u>In the U.S. today, church and state are legally separated.</u> Under our Constitution, government may neither establish nor prohibit the free exercise of religion. However, this does not mean that government does not acknowledge the existence of religious groups. Laws exist which seek to insure the separation of church and state and to protect the rights of each. Also, laws exist which regulate practices widely acknowledged to be dangerous to public safety, health, and general well-being—even if these practices are based on religious beliefs.

<u>While England may foster the well-being of a particular religious group, the United States assumes a position of neutrality.</u> Neither religion or nonreligion is espoused by the U.S. government.

5. Penn said, "Persecution makes men conform only because of outward force and bodily punishments. A faith enforced this way is subject to as many revolutions as the powers that enact it." How might Barton answer this charge?

Penn's charge could be answered in several ways. Barton could assume the position that there is only one true faith—his own. Rulers, therefore, are obliged to save fellowmen from false belief by any means, including force. He might also argue that persecution or restraint is only a "teacher." We hold the child out of danger, even against his will, until he learns that our judgments are best for him. Then force is no longer required. He might also argue that men who conform only out of fear must not be sincere in the first place—only hypocrites.

6. What effect might the granting of freedom of conscience in Pennsylvania have had on the subsequent development of religion in America?

Freedom of conscience was incorporated into the basic laws of America. Constitutional and ideological restrictions on establishment and government fostered religious conformity paved the way for the development of great religious diversity (pluralism) in America. Without freedom of conscience this would have been impossible. The full story of this diversity is told in another lesson.

CONTEMPORARY PARALLEL

One of the most popular phrases today is the term "life style." Its use, however, is usually in the plural—life-styles. Perhaps thinking about the different life-styles in our country today presents an appropriate contemporary parallel to the issue of conformity and diversity.

The Scranton Report on Campus Unrest concluded that "To most Americans the development of the new youth culture is an unpleasant and often frightening thing." Students can probably illustrate the threatening aspect of youth's nonconformity on the basis of their own experiences. Theodore Roszak, in his widely-quoted The Making of a Counter-Culture, comments on the nature of this threat: "For better or worse, most of what is presently happening that is new, provocative, and engaging in politics, education, the arts, social relations (love, family, courtship, community) is the creation either of youth who are profoundly, even fanatically, alienated from the parental generation, or of those who address themselves primarily to the young."

The diversity in our society, however, is not merely a division between the adult and youth cultures. Pluralism manifests itself in many significant ways, including the area of religion. Since religious pluralism will be the focus of a later study, perhaps the major emphasis in this study should be on the aspect of life-styles. For example, diversity is characteristic of the youth culture itself. Students can compare such terms as "beatniks," "hippies," "flower children," "new left," "militants," and "Jesus freaks." What life-styles do they represent? Is the criticism that young people simply conform in their nonconformity a valid one? Students might be interested in Charles Reich's provocative analysis of the clothes of the youth culture. He argues that blue jeans, for example, rather than being "uniform," are actually extremely expressive of the human body, and that each body is unique! Reich points out that whereas men's suits really are uniform in hiding the fact that one man may be muscular, another flabby, short, bony, hairy, or smooth, jeans actually take on the unique shape of the individual body and express the shape of the legs, heavy or thin, straight or bowed. According to Reich, "The new clothes deny the importance of hierarchy, status, authority, position, and they reject competition." In the context of the discussion of clothes, students could discuss the pro's and con's of attempts to establish dress codes in school.

One of the most interesting and threatening evidences of nonconformity in our society today is the emergence of different styles of family life. Much is being written and discussed about the future of the nuclear family, the impact of women's liberation, the need for an "extended family," and the search for simpler life-styles. A publication, entitled Alternatives, is devoted to a description of alternative life-styles, various experiments in communal living. Students might find a study of the communal life of the Hutterite religious sect (Montana) of particular interest in this regard. The lifestyle of the Amish sect and the continual struggle of this sect with the government is a fascinating model for the issue of religious conscience vs. public welfare. As students wrestle with these problems of diversity and conformity, they will be participating in one of the most difficult and significant aspects of a pluralistic society.

SUGGESTED ACTIVITIES

Questions for Further Thought:

1. Why, out of 40,000 inhabitants, are only 500 people in Lancaster County adherents to the Church of England?

Pennsylvania was a haven for people seeking religious freedom. It was more hospitable than, say, Massachusetts, where there was an established (Congregational) church. Thus greater diversity, as illustrated in Barton's letter, could be expected in this colony. In Virginia and other southern colonies, the Anglican Church was predominant.

2. Why, in attacking the claims of infallibility, does Penn emphasize Protestantism?

Infallibility was often ascribed to the judgments of the Pope as God's chief agent on earth. Thus, while a Catholic might ascribe infallibility to other than God, a Protestant normally would not.

3. Was Barton's suggestion that a law be passed obliging Germans to give their children an English education a reasonable one? Do you think newly arrived immigrants to the United States are under a similar obligation today? If so, why?

The suggestion of Barton that an English education be made compulsory is not unreasonable if this means learning those things essential to the well-being of the society. In the United States immigrants have been required to send their children to school to learn those things necessary to become a responsible member of society. Language, mathematics and social understandings have been seen as vital. However, if Barton meant indoctrination in the precepts of the Anglican Church, this would be unreasonable. All schools at this time were private and religiously oriented; the odds are, therefore, that Barton had in mind turning out good Anglicans. In his view, of course, this was equivalent to turning out good citizens.

4. Why might an Anglican, such as Barton, see in the various sects greater change in beliefs and practices than in his own religion?

Barton would see greater changes in sects which did not depend upon a hierarchy and tradition for the development of doctrine. The Church of England theologians could not proclaim changes upon inspiration as the leaders of sects might.

5. Barton observed that the Quakers viewed the Presbyterians of Pennsylvania with hostility. In light of the attitude of Penn, the Quaker founder of the colony, what might account for such an observation?

While individual Quakers might not reflect the ideals set by Penn and might openly resent Presbyterian competition, it is more likely that Barton's view of Quaker-Presbyterian relations was somewhat jaundiced. This could be expected of someone for whom toleration and diversity were unpleasant.

Suggestions for Further Research:

These areas of investigation are suggested for those students wishing to do additional research. In guiding students in their individual efforts, be sure to use the "Basic Library" as well as the Resource Guide below.

1. Can you discover anything about the Dunkers, New Lights, Covenanters, Brownists or Independents? Did these groups flourish only in the freedom of Penn's colony? Find out who they were, what they believed and if there survive today any descendants in contemporary groups.

2. If England persecuted the Quakers, how was Penn able to acquire a huge grant of land for a colony? What reasons did the English Crown have for doing this?

3. Penn wrote his book in 1670. From that point trace the development of the official English attitude on toleration. When did it change, and why?

4. What is Barton talking about when he speaks simply of "the church"? Would Quakers be in any sense part of "the church"? Where did this concept originate?

VOCABULARY

accountable	defile	impeach
Caesar	disposition	infallible
civil authority	diversity	meddle
coercion	fanaticism	persecution
conformity		

RESOURCE GUIDE FOR STUDY 2

I. Audio Visual Aids

A. Films

Barbara-To Conform or not to Conform. 6½ min., Color, rental: Varies (approx.: $6.00)
New York University, New York, New York
Barbara, a little girl, discovers conformity and nonconformity in a role as a leader. Confused, she finally consults her uncle who helps her realize she is most happy and distinguished when she is herself.

Conformity. 49 min., b&w. Produced by WCAU-TV, Philadelphia, 1964.
Available on loan from Sterling Educational Film, 241 E. 34th St., New York, N. Y. 10016
Explores the ways in which an individual can fall into conformity in modern society. This film could spark controversy and should be used only with mature students.

The Hutterites. 28 min., b&w, rental: $12.50
Sterling Educational Films, 241 E. 34th St., New York, N. Y. 10016
This film traces the history and characteristics of the Hutterites, one of three Anabaptist groups surviving from the Reformation period. Showing the group in west Canada, the film describes the religious beliefs, manner of living, educational policies, farming practices and their entire manner of

life in "complete community." Recommended. As examples of "nonconformity" this and the following film could well serve to introduce the religious issue. Of course, one must point out that these are extreme cases involving partial withdrawal from the larger society.

The Old Order Amish. 33 min., Color, Rental: $15.00
    Vedo Films, 85 Longview Rd., Port Washington, N.Y. 11050
This film is about how the Amish of the Pennsylvania Dutch country turn their backs on the world and progress in order to practice the virtues of holiness, humility and hard work. Communal efforts in the areas of housework, farming and building construction reveal the cooperation existing within the Amish community. It concludes on the note that increasing difficulties with outside life may weaken the Amish society.

Salem Witch Trials. 27 min., b&w, rental: $5.75
    McGraw Hill (Text-film department), 330 W. 42nd St., New York, N. Y. 10036
In the Salem Colony, August, 1692, mass hysteria makes "witches" of innocent people. You might develop an activity comparing the Salem experience with contemporary hostilities stimulated by "nonconformity."

William Penn and the Quakers. 11 min., color or b&w, rental rates vary
    Coronet Films, 65 E. South Water St., Chicago, Illinois 60601
This film shows the Quaker's religious struggle in the 17th century England. Shows the founding of the colony under William Penn, who was dedicated to freedom of speech, religion, and equality to all. The film also shows how this colony developed to be a leader among the original colonies.

II. Articles

"Age of the Person," Seventeen, volume 26 (December, 1967).

"The Hutterites, Plain People of the West," National Geographic, volume 138 (July, 1970).

"A Kind Word for Conformity: American Life in the 1960's" Saturday Review, volume 48 (December 11, 1965).

III. Books

Andrews, Edward D. The Gift to be Simple. New York: Dover Publications (paper) $2.00 Songs and rituals of the Shaker community. Written music and bibliography for recordings.

Bacon, Margaret H. The Quiet Rebels: The Story of the Quakers in America. New York: Basic Books, 1969. $5.95

"The Church Confronts Loyalty and Dissent." America, volume 122 (June 27, 1970). Nine articles.

Dunn, Mary M. William Penn: Politics and Conscience. Princeton: Princeton University Press. $6.00

Elgin, Kathleen. The Quakers. New York: David McKay Company. $4.50

Hostetler, John A. Amish Life. Revised edition Scottdale, Pennsylvania Herald Press (paper) $.50

_____. Hutterite Life. Scottdale, Pennsylvania Herald Press (paper) $.50

Hostetler, John A. Mennonite Life. Revised edition Scottdale, Pennsylvania: Herald Press. (paper) $.50

_____ and Huntington, Gertrude E. Hutterites in North America. New York: Holt, Rinehart and Winston. (paper) $1.95

Jordan, Mildred. Proud to be Amish. New York: Crown $3.50

Meryman, Richard S., Jr. "South Dakota's Christian Martyrs" [Harper's Magazine, December, 1958] chapter 18 in Andrew M. Scott and Earle Wallace, Politics, U.S.A.: Cases on the American Democratic Process. New York: MacMillan, (paper) $4.95

Myers, Gustavus. History of Bigotry in the United States. New York: Putnam (Capricorn). (paper) $2.25

Peare, Catherine O. John Woolman: Child of Light. New York: Vanguard Press. $3.95

Peattie, Donald C. "Pioneer of Freedom," in Great Lives, Great Deeds. Reader's Digest Association. An enjoyable and easy essay on William Penn.

Rapson, Richard L. Individualism and Conformity in the American Character. Indianapolis: D. C. Heath. (paper) $2.25

Stevenson, W. C. The Inside Story of Jehovah's Witnesses. New York: Hart Publishing Company. $5.95

Turner, Wallace. The Mormon Establishment. Boston: Houghton Mifflin. $6.00

(In the Basic Library, particular attention is called to the following volumes:

Brauer, Protestantism in America

Ellis, American Catholicism

Hudson, Religion in America

Stokes & Pfeffer, Church and State in the United States

Sweet, Religion in Colonial America)

3

THE AMERICAN REVOLUTION: A RELIGIOUS WAR?

THE PLAN OF STUDY

Introduction

Thomas Bradbury Chandler, "An Appeal to the Public"

William Livingston, "A Letter to the Bishop of Landaff"

Contemporary Parallel

Some Suggested Activities

Vocabulary

Resource Guide

THE FOCUS OF THIS STUDY

This study presents students with information about religious issues in the American Revolution. A "religious war" is one in which ideological or ecclesiastical questions are primary sources of conflict. However, in other cases religious issues may be hidden, being closely interwoven with those of a political, social or economic nature.

The study is designed to be part of a unit dealing with the causes of the Revolution. Thus it should complement and complete a study dealing with events leading to the nation's independence.

But beyond the historical case of revolution, the Study raises questions about the nature of authority and its legitimate basis in a group or society. What "makes" authority and gives it power, say, in government, in religious institutions, and in the family. In a conflict situation, where an actor has goals and needs conflicting with the authority, what is his proper course of action? In a similar situation for a group what is its proper course of action? When is a break with authority justified? And when is a violent break (such as rebellion) justified? Today, as American society wrestles with problems concerning authority and a constant questioning of traditional authority, students' study of this issue seems both relevant and useful. Another enduring, fundamental question raised by the Study concerns the relationship between religious and civil liberty. Is one derived from the other? Is one essential to the other?

OBJECTIVES FOR THIS STUDY

Knowledge Objectives—Each student will demonstrate his knowledge that:

1. Religious motives played an important role in the actions of the patriots in the Revolutionary War era, and religious motives have played, and continue to play, a role in issues involving authority.

2. The question of sending bishops to America was part of the general problem in Anglo-American relations on the eve of the American Revolution.

3. A "religious" issue may involve both religious and secular questions.

4. A multiplicity of causes lay behind the American Revolution, and no single factor explanation seems valid as an explanation of that revolution or as an explanation or predictor for other rebellions and revolutions.

Skill Objectives—Each student will demonstrate his ability to:

1. Define central issues from a set of brief quotations.

2. Distinguish between religious-issue positions based upon theology and those based upon non-theological considerations (i.e., politics, economics).

3. Test reasons and generalizations about "why rebellions and revolutions occur," which were held upon beginning study, with evidence about the occurrence of the American Revolution, then, using such generalizations to hypothesize about contemporary rebellion and the questioning of authority.

4. State reasons as normative principles to justify courses of action relative to authority, to justify those principles in the historical context, and to extend them to contemporary situations for further testing and justification.

Attitude and Value Objectives—Each student will demonstrate his willingness to:

1. Analyze religiously biased materials for data and for skill development.

2. Confront emotionally charged historic and contemporary issues with an open mind toward evidence and dissonance-producing positions presented by other classmates and informants.

3. Use the study of controversial issues to clarify and evaluate his value commitments as they apply to concrete situations.

4. Develop an intellectual curiosity which enables him to analyze issues rationally, applying appropriate skills, and considering his own emotions and value commitments, without accepting the two extremes of 1) unquestioning acceptance of what he reads and hears and 2) cynical rejection of evidence, no matter what the source.

INTRODUCTION

To begin the study, direct students to read the five quotations—and no more. Have them examine the questions following the quotations. Then hold a short discussion. The purpose of this first discussion is to draw out student impressions of "what's going on?" Have students speculate about what has aroused the five men to speak out. When students offer hypotheses concerning colonists fear of Anglican bishops coming to America, ask why bishops might be feared. When discussing the multiple-choice question, point out that none of the men were anti-religious. They were in agreement in opposing bishops, but some did so for theological reasons, some for fear of losing their political liberty.

Students should appreciate the bitterness, open hostility and magnitude of the controversy in observing that those opposed to bishops did not enjoy freedom publicly to voice their position. Even in large cities such as New York and Philadelphia, men feared reprisals and found it prudent to use false names.

Have students read the rest of the Introduction. You might ask: Does the statement of John Adams help explain the quotations and the motives of the men who wrote them?

THOMAS BRADBURY CHANDLER

Upon completing the introductory discussion, assign the primary source readings of Chandler and Livingston. Point out to students that these readings will help them test their hypotheses concerning "What's going on?" Guiding questions direct students to significant points in the readings. No discussion is planned on each reading. However, if you wish to help individual students with the guiding questions, consider the following.

1. What objections did Americans raise to having Anglican bishops in "this country"? How did Chandler react to these objections?

Some Americans feared they would be taxed to support the bishops. This was the case in England. Chandler said this would not be the case in America, for a special fund has been set up to support the bishops. However, he does indicate that good members of a society should not object to a small tax.

Also, colonists feared that civil and religious liberties might be curtailed. Some felt that the bishops would gradually add political power to their church authority. Chandler said that no denomination would suffer. Further, he argues, if bishops were granted "some degree" of civil authority (as they had in England) it is "inconceivable that any would thereby be injured."

Have students relate what they already know about events leading up to the Revolution to information in this reading.

Colonists were concerned about the loss of civil liberties, but also they recognized how civil and religious liberty were so closely tied together in eighteenth-century England.

2. What is Chandler's "political argument" for importing bishops? Would any Americans be impressed by this position? Why? Why not?

Chandler argues that episcopacy (government by bishops) and the civil constitution (of England) support each other. He feels that no form of church government can so exactly harmonize with constitutional monarchy as the episcopacy found in the Church of England. Since many colonists were unhappy with the very government that Chandler praises, they would hardly be impressed with his reasoning that bishops should be accepted because they harmonize with that government.

WILLIAM LIVINGSTON

When helping individual students with the Livingston reading, consider the following.

1. How does Livingston view the state of religion in America compared with England?

Livingston believes that the colonies surpass England "both in the theory and practice of Christianity." He further notes that "there never was a people in the world who have been more earnest in preserving their native religion and in transmitting it, pure and uncorrupt, to their posterity." As far as Livingston is concerned, "there is not a more virtuous, not a more religious people upon the face of the earth."

2. What does Livingston find wrong with religion in England? (The "wrongs" he believes Americans have left behind.)

Livingston sees as wrongs in England's religion (1) submission to arbitrary and tyrannical ecclesiastical political power, (2) recognition of a man as supreme head of the church, and (3) superstitious attachment to rites and ceremonies of human invention.

3. What need, then, would there be for bishops to come to America according to Livingston?

There is no need, implies Livingston, for bishops to come to America since religion without bishops is in better condition than religion with bishops.

Note: You might point out that Livingston was a Presbyterian. As such, he would be unalterably opposed to bishops on theological grounds even if he lived in England. He obviously would be proud of the Calvinist strongholds in Switzerland, Holland, and Scotland.

Students should realize that Livingston's letter was a "public letter," a humorous and sarcastic piece written for publication in the press. Ask students to locate his barbs and the function of this wit in helping to affect public opinion in the colonies. Students might also consider examples of this style in today's newspapers and the effectiveness of this technique.

1. If you were an American colonist of 1768 and read the arguments of both Chandler and Livingston, which would impress you as the better written?

If colonists in America were fearful of ecclesiastical authority, Chandler's "appeal" would certainly not put their minds to rest. He makes light of the colonists' objections as he tells them their fears are groundless. His bland assertion that bishops are always "possessed of the greatest abilities, integrity and prudence" is obviously unjustified. Finally, his advocacy of a church "interwoven with the civil constitution" and supporting monarchy would be especially distasteful to those Americans resenting the oppressive measures of George III's government.

Livingston supports his argument against bishops by pointing out the superiority of Christian theory and practice where no bishops exist (America, Holland, Switzerland and Scotland). He indicates that Christianity may be rendered unpure and corrupt through ecclesiastical authority. Livingston's writing appealed particularly to non-Anglicans and to those Americans growing restless under any show of English authority.

2. Drawing upon the original sources in this lesson, what argument could be made about the relationship between ecclesiastic and civil authority?

It is obvious from the 1768 "letters" that the colonists feared loss of liberty through the bishops' use of their civil authority. Chandler, too, indicates that churchmen may be judicial officers. In England, episcopacy and civil authority were wedded. It was assumed that this would be the case in the American colonies.

3. How would this argument help explain the opposition to bishops by American patriots in the 1760's?

In the 1760's, American patriots were increasingly voicing oppostion to what they felt was the arbitrary authority of the crown. Attempts to import bishops were seen as a move to retain or extend that authority. The class here might review some of the political and economic actions that were increasing resentment among the colonists. It is important in this lesson to keep the chronology of events before the student's attention. For the events soon build a momentum of their own.

4. In the colonial mind, how might fear of England's ecclesiastical powers be related to fears of her political and economic powers? Is this a reasonable relationship to draw? Why? Why not?

Under a generalized fear of English power could be found fears that were ecclesiastical or political or economic. The average colonist may not have made a distinction among them. They were all simply manifestations of English might. A fear of ecclesiastical power, by itself, could hardly have tripped the American Revolution. But added to all the other fears in the air <u>at this time</u>, the religious issue is a most significant one.

5. Given the "causes" of the American Revolution which you can find using the school library collection, the textbook, and this Study, do you think that the patriots were justified in seeking independence from Great Britian by violent means? If not, what could justify a rebellion or revolution in this situation? If so, what principles can you state that warrant your conclusion that revolution was justified?

The teacher should conduct guided discussion on these open-ended questions, carefully getting students to state their conclusions, stated as principles ("A revolution is justified on the part of the patriots if they were taxed without participating in the taxing authority through representatives: participation and rational consent being necessary for authority to be legitimate and its decisions binding." "The patriots were justified in rebelling against the imposition of bishops, because. . . ."). With principles stated, the teacher may pose probing questions to obtain "reasons behind the reasons" from students—why are these principles valid? When students feel that they have justified the principles and are satisfied, the teacher might move to the contemporary parallel section and see if students will transfer, modify, or reject the principles as warranting rebellion and resistance to authority on the contemporary scene.

CONTEMPORARY PARALLEL

This study raises the issue of the relationship between religious and political authority, and, by implication, the relationship between civil and religious liberties. One contemporary example of this conflict is the State of Israel. The Chief Rabbinate in Israel is a state institution entrusted with many state functions, such as cases of family law when Jews are involved. Because the Rabbinate has been strictly Orthodox, it has used every conceivable weapon, especially political pressures, against the establishment of non-Orthodox Jewish congregations in Israel. Jewish theologian Leo Trepp sees this situation as responsible for the fact that "Israeli Jews in their majority have no religion." Trepp suggests that a separation of church and state in Israel would be in the interest of religion itself, arguing "Not only would it give full freedom of development to all Jewish religious groups in Israel, but it might also lead the Rabbinate into the creative contest of ideas, thereby revitalizing it to the benefit of all."

Another modern-day example of religious-political conflict is the sporadic, bloody warfare between Catholics and Protestants in Northern Ireland, where these two religious groups are fighting over economic and social privileges, political status, and ties with the neighboring Irish Republic (predominantly Catholic). This situation poses unusually complex interrelationships between political and religious authorities. For example, James Chichester-Clark, former Prime Minister and leader of the moderate Protestants, was recently ousted by right-wing Protestants in his own party who oppose all efforts to secure social and political emancipation of the Catholic minority. Students may recall the recent visit to this country by Bernadette Devlin, fiery Catholic civil-rights worker and member of the British parliament, who has dramatized the issues of the Northern Ireland conflict to the American public.

Church-state conflict in Argentina was revealed most recently in an Argentine army report denouncing a progressive priests' movement as "revolutionary and subversive" and a clerical group's condemnation of a government colonization plan as exploiting the working and rural classes for the purpose of "materialistic development." These charges have heightened the tensions between the country's two most powerful institutions.

A much-publicized example of the conflict of religious and civil authority in the United States is the case of the Berrigan brothers, priests who were arrested and imprisoned for burning three hundred files of draft cards with home-made napalm. They maintained their motive was to dramatize "how wantonly lives have been squandered in Asia—with no one punished for doing so; whereas we get stiff sentences for trying to highlight the tragedy by burning up government paper."

Students might be asked to find the implications in the following commentary by Edward Duff, American Catholic priest and political scientist: "The example of the Berrigans raises the doubt that American Catholicism can be counted on to supply acolytes for all the shrines of the civic religion that is the American Way of Life. . . . The ultimate scandal for the Jesuit-graduate FBI agent who arrested Father Berrigan . . . was the fact of a priest defying the government."

These four illustrations open up large areas for investigation, for discussion, and for judgment making in the important issue of religious-political conflict.

SOME SUGGESTED ACTIVITIES

Two Brief Essays

These questions are designed to help students hypothesize about succeeding events. Later, these hypotheses may be tested by further historical investigation. Have each student compose two one-page essays. If you wish to hold a discussion of the hypotheses offered, point out the following:

1. How would you expect Chandler and most colonial Anglican clergy to "line up" at the time of the American Revolution? Tory or Patriot? Why?

Many of the Anglican clergy were not permanent residents of America. They were missionaries here without family or home ties so that their loyalties were directed toward England. In the Southern colonies, however, a large number of Anglicans supported the Revolution.

2. After the Revolution, America did have bishops. How much difference did independence make?

All the difference is made when there is no real fear of authority. Without an "establishment" of the Anglican Church, episcopal powers were limited to leadership of but one denomination in America. Being loyal Americans, these later bishops were not open to charges of intrigue on behalf of Britain. Also, of course, after the Revolution, there were the Constitutional safeguards.

Suggestions for Further Research

These areas of investigation are suggested for those students wishing to do additional research. In guiding students in their individual efforts, be sure to use the "Basic Library" as well as the Resource Guide below.

1. Chandler contended that episcopacy could never thrive in a republic. Yet, today, we do have bishops in America.

   a. What churches in the U.S. today have bishops?
   b. What kinds of authority do these bishops have that is different from or similar to that held by Anglican bishops of the 18th century?

2. Various religious groups responded to the American Revolution in different ways. What was the position of (a) Presbyterians, (b) Quakers, and (c) Anglicans?

VOCABULARY

affirm	burdensome	infatuated	posterity
arbitrary	commodity	inoffensive	preeminence
authentic	defiled	integrity	prudence
bask	encroachment	invest (with authority)	republic

RESOURCE GUIDE FOR STUDY 3

I. Audio Visual Aids

A. Films

American Revolution: The Background Period. 11 min., b&w, rental: $2.25
   Coronet Films, 65 E. South Water St., Chicago, Ill. 60601
Treats the political, social, and economic conditions that formed the background of the American Revolution, and those events which forced the colonists to rebel. This film might be used to develop a frame of reference for studying the religious factors in the move for independence.

The Rebel. 28 min., b&w, rental rates vary
   Birad Corporation, 1564 Broadway, New York, N.Y. 10036
Set in the days of the American Revolution, this film is the story of Rabbi Seixas. It portrays his part in throwing off the yoke of Colonialism showing the influence of his dramatic stand on the colonies.

The Red Box. 30 min. Eternal Light (kinescope). $8.50
   An episode in the life of Gershom Seixas, a rabbi who lived during the American Revolution and fought for religious freedom.

II. Articles

"Bishops and Protestant Unity: Episcopacy Issue," America, volume 114 (May 14, 1966).

"Freedom Beyond Polity: Is Episcopacy the Answer?" Christian Century, volume 82 (November 10, 1965).

The two articles above illustrate how episcopacy is still a live issue.

"The Political Rights of the Jews in the United States; 1776–1840." American Jewish Archives (Hebrew Union College–Jewish Institute of Religion, Cincinnati) volume 10 (April 1958).

"Sons of Liberty," Reader's Digest, volume 87 (November, 1965).

III. Books

Akers, Charles W. Called Unto Liberty: A Life of Jonathan Mayhew, 1720–1766. Cambridge: Harvard University Press. $6.50

Bridenbaugh, Carl. Mitre and Sceptre. New York: Oxford University Press. $1.95
The basic volume for this lesson, providing detailed and essential demonstration of the role of religion in the Revolutionary Period.

Catton, Bruce, editor. The American Heritage Book of the Revolution. New York: Simon & Schuster. $12.50

Fast, Howard M. Haym Solomon, Son of Liberty. New York: Messner. $3.95 Fictionalized biography of the Polish immigrant Jew and his involvement with the American Revolution.

Feuerlicht, Morris M. Judaism's Influence in the Founding of the Republic. The Commission on Information About Judaism, 838 Fifth Avenue, New York, New York 10021. (Booklet)

Lomask, Milton. John Carroll: Bishop and Patriot. New York: Farrar, Strauss and Giroux (Vision). $2.95

(In the Basic Library, particular attention is called to the following volumes:

Mead, The Lively Experiment

Stokes & Pfeffer, Church and State in the United States)

4

SUBSIDY OR SEPARATION?

THE PLAN OF THE STUDY

Introduction

Founding Fathers Disagree on Subsidy for Religion

Tax Exemptions for the Churches: A. P. Stokes and Leo Pfeffer

The Churches Speak: Four Points of View

A Summary of Arguments

The Supreme Court Speaks

The Case of "Middletown"

Contemporary Parallel

Suggested Activities

Vocabulary

Resource Guide

THE FOCUS FOR THIS STUDY

In this study students are presented with and asked to clarify the complex nature of church-state economic relations. Since the fourth-century patronage of Emperor Constantine, churches have enjoyed a favored status in Western civilization. When seen as an agent of government, the church is obviously entitled to support by tax revenue. As a corollary, the church was freed of tax obligations. With the American Revolution, however, "establishment" of religion by financial support is challenged and eventually thrown out. The second step, though, was not taken: tax exemptions have remained to the present. Recently, this, too, has been challenged, and the U.S. Supreme Court in 1970 turned its attention to this question.

When studying this issue, students can learn important skills in coping with public issues and in decision-making. They will analyze and evaluate several position papers and arguments on the issue, interact with their classmates who will have arguments to make, and finally, make their own judgment and supporting argument. During this process, students will have the opportunity to confront diverse alternative positions and to clarify their values relative to the tax exemption issue in particular, and church-state issues in general.

THE OBJECTIVES FOR THIS STUDY

<u>Knowledge Objectives</u>—Each student will demonstrate his knowledge that:

1. The finances of churches and the economics of government are inextricably interwoven, and the increasing economic pressure upon government for sustained and improved services (and thus, pressures on the taxpayers) has brought active public discussion on the issue of tax exemption.

2. Basic issues of church-state relations, problematic to the Founding Fathers, remain so today.

3. The religious community is not of one mind on these church-state issues.

4. Theological and practical considerations, as well as constitutional, are weighted in developing a posture on church-state relations.

5. Government policy greatly affects the fate of organized religion.

6. There are sets of arguments for and against the tax exemption policy, and to know several reasons given on each side.

<u>Skill Objectives</u>—Each student will demonstrate his ability to:

1. Identify a position and its warranting argument in a public position paper by religious organizations and in documents expressing individual judgments.

2. Analyze and evaluate those arguments, locating implicit assumptions and judging the creditability and sufficiency of the evidence grounding the judgment, or the reasons warranting a value judgment.

3. Relate value judgments expressed in historical materials of different periods to a continuing issue in American history.

4. Develop hypotheses and gather evidence to test it, regarding the effects of continued government subsidy of religion.

<u>Value and Attitude Objectives</u>—Each student will demonstrate his willingness to:

1. Discuss issues potentially challenging to personal commitments and to evaluate his position on the issues rationally and openly in concert with his teacher and classmates.

2. Respect viewpoints dissimilar to his own, expressed by classmates and by authors of various readings, while requesting reasonable justification and participating in argumentation.

INTRODUCTION

Students are introduced to the issue by being reminded that <u>some problems do not have simple, permanent solutions. The central theme is whether or not there is justification for governmental support or subsidy of religion.</u>

FOUNDING FATHERS DISAGREE ON SUBSIDY FOR RELIGION

What <u>did</u> the founding fathers mean when they wrote the First Amendment? One way to resolve this question is to read the founders on this subject. Two primary historical sources are presented in this section.

Patrick Henry

Patrick Henry's bill clearly shows the thinking of one American patriot. Questions are provided to guide students to significant points. No discussion of these is planned; however, if you help individuals with the reading, the following should be considered.

1. How does Henry attempt to use the government to impose orthodoxy in religion?

Henry not only wishes to "establish" Christianity, but also to insure conformity. He indicates conditions to be met by groups and ministers before they may be considered legal. An unorthodox group would not receive any of the tax monies.

2. How does Henry's bill tend to discourage the development of new sects or denominations?

This necessity for official approval would in itself discourage the development of new sects. Additionally, the requirement that a minister be chosen by a majority of the society would discourage splinter movements.

3. What provision is made for the person not wishing to belong to a church organization?

Henry has no place in his scheme for the nonbeliever or agnostic.

James Madison

James Madison is revealed, in his "Memorial and Remonstrance," as a staunch advocate of freedom of conscience. No discussion of the guiding questions is planned; however, when helping individuals with this reading, the following should be considered.

1. How does Madison show his opposition to achieving religious conformity through authority? What are his reasons?

<u>Religion is exempt from the authority of society</u> and, thus, of a legislative body. <u>Religion involves a duty owed only to God.</u> The manner in which this <u>duty is discharged is directed by conviction and not by force.</u>

2. What is meant by taking "alarm at the first experiment on our liberties"? What is a "prudent jealousy"?

Madison warns that Henry's bill may be but a "foot in the door." After this, greater abuses will follow and eventually all liberties may be lost.

3. What, in Madison's opinion, does history teach us about "established churches" in the past? What evidence does he offer? Do you know of other historical data that would tend to support or refute his position?

Establishment, says Madison, has always worked against true religion. Corruption and persecution follow establishment and the purity and efficacy of religion disappear.

TAX EXEMPTIONS FOR THE CHURCHES

Tax exemptions granted to synagogues and churches is the other side of the coin. Indirect subsidy rather than direct payment is the contemporary issue. Not being subject to taxation, a church may enhance its relative financial standing as though it had received a direct payment. But the picture is a complex one: while direct payments to support religion can be seen clearly as an "establishment," tax exemption is often viewed as an example of separation. Indeed, for some observers taxation would imply control of the church by the state.

As local governments are sorely pressed to find new sources of revenue, they gaze covetously upon church property not now on tax rolls. Also, as church holdings increase, those persons burdened with rising income taxes demand the elimination of loopholes. The special position of the churches vis-a-vis the American economy thus undergoes continued scrutiny.

In the article by Stokes and Pfeffer, various aspects of the exemption issue are revealed. Students should understand the difference between locally levied property taxes and federal (or state) income taxes. As the church buys land, this land is removed from the local tax base. An extra burden must be assumed by other owners of private property, and opposition therefore arises. Exemption from corporate income tax, moreover, can be seen as a denial of the concept of separation of church and state and as an unfair advantage enjoyed by the churches in competition with secular enterprises. In addition, church-member critics of exemptions have pointed out that over-concern for money can cause the churches to lose sight of their mission.

Since the Stokes-Pfeffer reading does not fully treat this issue, you may wish to insert additional information at this point in the study. Suggestions are provided in the resource guide for this study. Especially recommended is the "CBS Report" film, The Business of Religion. A good background source for the teacher is found in The Religious Situation: 1968.[1]

THE CHURCHES SPEAK: FOUR POINTS OF VIEW

These four readings reflect divergent views on the tax exemption question. Students should know that the churches do not speak with one voice on this issue. Further, within the various churches considerable disagreement exists. Students should be able to articulate each of the arguments. Also, they should be prepared to judge the validity of the arguments.

America

The editorial from America presents one Catholic viewpoint. It concludes that very little revenue would be gained from taxing the churches. If students need help with the guiding questions, the following should be considered.

1. Why would the government gain no money from a tax on church income?

---

[1] Guild of St. Ives, "A Report on Churches and Taxation" in Donald R. Cutler (ed.) The Religious Situation: 1968. (New York: Beacon Press, 1968), pp. 931–960.

America states that the churches have very little taxable income. First, the greatest part of their income is from free-will offerings, nontaxable as gifts. Second, the churches' oridinary and necessary expenses would use up any potentially taxable income from other sources. Thus, little taxable income would be left.

2. Why would a tax on church property bring little revenue?

A tax on church property would bring little revenue. First, some church property, such as schools and hospitals, are entitled to exemption regardless of their religious affiliation. Second, an assessment of property on which houses of worship stand would be difficult because there is no basis for assessing the economic value of religion. Because religion is not profit-making, little tax money would be realized even if a basis for assessment were developed.

3. Are these good arguments?

Students can evaluate the arguments by their logical consistency: "Do the reasons given relate to the main assertion?"; by the prediction of consequences: "Is it likely that these consequences would follow from this policy? What evidence do we have to accept these probable consequences?"; and by the value placed upon the consequences: "If this will happen if we do that, is this desirable?" Undesirable? Why? Why not?"

General Assembly, United Presbyterian Church, U.S.A.

The United Presbyterian Church statement contains theological and practical reasons why tax exemptions may weaken the church. The guiding questions raise the following considerations.

1. What does "ambiguous witness" mean?

A "conflict of interest" charge could cloud the churches' testimony of the truth of the gospel. An analogy might be drawn with the judge who presides in a case in which he has a vested interest. A church's witness would be less ambiguous if it maintained its independence.

2. What is meant by "quid pro quo"—especially in this context?

The church may be placed in a quid pro quo (literally, this for that) situation by accepting favored status from the government. By accepting such status, is the church thus constrained to aid and not criticize the state in return? Patrick Henry, it may be noted, saw such a situation as a natural state of affairs. "No person whatsoever shall speak anything in their Religious Assemblies disrespectfully or Seditiously of the Government of this State."

3. How do these two factors affect the churches' mission or work?

To be effective the church must maintain an undiluted loyalty to Christ. The teaching of the church must be based on religious authority alone. Only in this way can the church involve itself in temporal concerns, maintain its objectivity, and be the respected judge of society. If the church accepts favors from society, it may compromise its principles. Even if the church does not compromise, it may lose the respect of those who see the possibility of compromise.

Ave Maria

The periodical Ave Maria presents another Roman Catholic viewpoint. Also, the article raises some side issues. In treating the guiding questions consider the following.

1. Why might Congressmen be reluctant to condemn tax exemption for religious organizations?

Congressmen, as well as other elected officials, are loathe to take a stand against tax exemptions for churches. No one wants to appear to be antireligious. Thus congressmen might defend exemptions rather than endanger their popularity.

2. What ethical considerations are involved in this taxation question?

Church administrators should be concerned about whether exemptions are legitimate or are merely tax dodges. If churches are abusing their favored status and enjoying unfair advantage, this is a scandal.

3. If churches are required to pay all taxes, what might be the result?

Churches may have to curtail their social services if they are required to pay all taxes. This, then, would place additional responsibility on the government. Consequently, the individual taxpayer would not see his tax bill reduced.

General Convention, American Church

The Lutheran statement presents specific policy positions on various aspects of the tax exemption issue. In treating the guiding questions, consider the following.

1. How can tax policies or tax law encourage persons to give to churches and synagogues?

By allowing religious contributions to be liberally deducted from personal income tax assessments, tax laws encourage such contributions. Also, if church organizations pay their fair share, personal income tax might be lowered—again encouraging contributions. The money thus received by the churches can be spent on public service relieving the government of some burden. This gives the individual more influence over how his money is to be spent than if it went into the general revenue.

2. What kind of tax exemption should churches have? What kind should they not have?

Church property that is used directly for charitable, educational and worship activities should be exempt from taxation. Churches should, however, pay for public services. Churches should pay taxes on dwellings owned by them in which clergy and other members of religious organizations may reside. Church-owned businesses and properties not directly related to the above activities should be taxed the same as secularly owned enterprises.

A SUMMARY OF ARGUMENTS

This brief reading and the two study questions pull together the variety of positions relating to the tax exemption issue. To prepare for class discussion students should 1) review their notes, 2) answer the study questions for the reading, and 3) write out their positions with notes on the supporting arguments.

THE SUPREME COURT SPEAKS

Following the consideration of the students' positions and justification, they can compare their positions with the facts and the Court's decision in a recent case on the tax exemption issue.

1. Do you agree with the Court's understanding of the "basic purpose" of the First Amendment? Explain your answer.

The Court's understanding is one of "benevolent neutrality" whereby "the autonomy and freedom of religious bodies" is preserved "while avoiding any semblance of established religion." While government functions on this "tightrope," it cannot rigidly establish principles for all occasions. The students, however, might discuss what "benevolent neutrality" means on various situations which come to their minds.

2. What do you understand by the phrase "benevolent neutrality"? Does this seem reasonable to you as a path for the country to try and follow—or not?

Using their agreement or disagreement on Question 1 and their discussions on various situations in addition to the Waltz case, the students can decide upon the "reasonableness" of this concept.

3. Would you expect other cases involving tax money and religion to come before the Supreme Court? Why or why not?

By the time students get to this question in their discussion, they will probably realize that the "room for play in the joints productive of a benevolent neutrality" is sufficiently vague to prompt additional cases before the Court.

THE CASE OF "MIDDLETOWN"

This activity places each student in the dual role of tax-paying citizen and dues-paying church member. Because an individual in America plays multiple roles—he may be a neighbor, a parent, a home owner, a Jew, a union-member, a Republican, a Reserve officer, a civil-libertarian, and a part-time student—he is often faced with decisions in which his own best interests are not clear to him. For example, his interests as a union-member may conflict with his interests as a Republican. He must then weigh carefully all the factors that are to be considered. He must examine alternatives and try to foresee the results of various courses of action. Only then can he make an intelligent decision.

In this discussion—which can be teacher-led—students should draw on information from all the readings. They should offer possible solutions to the problem and rationally defend the efficacy of their solutions. As a number of solutions are possible and plausible, no attempt should be made to enforce agreement on a single solution. Each alternative should be explored, challenged, defended, and tentatively rejected or accepted as a possible course of action.

An alternate format might utilize a panel of experts. Superior students having undertaken additional preparation could lead the discussion. They could offer their own carefully worked out solution. The rest of the class might then use this as a point of departure for discussion. In either format, all students should be given the opportunity to state and defend their own convictions.

CONTEMPORARY PARALLEL

This study already incorporates a significant contemporary parallel in the issue of tax exemption for churches. However, students should be aware of other issues that involve the "financial wall" between church and state. Only two of the issues have received definitive treatment by the United States Supreme Court: the textbook problem and the transportation problem. The most famous decision in this area was the Everson Case (1947) in which the Court concluded that public funds for bus transportation of children attending Roman Catholic parochial schools did not constitute an establishment of religion because such funds aided the students rather than religion per se. This same "child benefit" theory was the basis for the Court's decision in 1930 permitting tax appropriations for textbooks in sectarian schools.

What should be the place of the parochial school in our country's education structure? Mary Perkins Ryan created a lively stir in 1964 with the publication of a brief tract entitled Are Parochial Schools the Answer? In the tract she criticized the "siege mentality" of the Catholic education ideal—every Catholic child in a Catholic school. On the other hand, other educators remind us that what the American public educational system most needs is hard-nosed competition. They urge that in the interest of educational reform, Protestant Christians should forget their fear of the Catholic hierarchy, repudiate the unholy alliance between the Protestant establishment and public education, and begin to push for the development of alternative educational systems—all of which should get a share of tax revenues, but in terms of subsidization of the student rather than of the school.

Clearly, the most persistent and troublesome question of all concerns whether or not federal aid to education should include aid to parochial schools. Although such aid is taken for granted in higher education where church-supported colleges receive public revenues, such aid has been staunchly resisted at the elementary and high school levels. The rationale has included the fact that colleges are above the compulsory school age limit; also, such bills provide that grants and loans not be used for divinity schools, chapels, or rooms devoted primarily to religious instruction.

The major objection to the use of public funds to parochial schools is the fear that such aid would constitute an establishment of religion and violate the separation of church and state. In regard to the textbook situation, for example, a study of textbooks used in parochial schools (subsequently published in the Harvard Educational Review) indicated that religion is integrated into virtually all parochial school texts, including science, language, and mathematics texts. Theologian-educator Robert Lynn, while appreciating such problems, is more concerned that Protestants fail to sense the interconnection between church-state issues and other policy goals, especially the process of desegregating urban public schools, and federal aid to education. He points out that the church-state issue of aid to parochial schools has served as the number one obstacle to federal aid to education.

Students might consider the following questions proposed by Rabbi Arthur Gilbert:

> Are we prepared to write off 12 per cent of our children as excluded from our concern? Can America afford such a waste? Is it not possible, therefore, to provide educational services for all children without regard to the school they attend; or train all teachers without regard to the uniform they wear; or provide laboratories and workshops, testing facilities as well as health and medical benefits and textbooks and transportation for all children without involving the Government in direct aid to one religion over another?[1]

The issue of subsidy or separation promises to be with us for a long time!

---

[1] Arthur Gilbert, "American Public Education and the Challenge of Religious Pluralism" (a talk at an Institute on Religion and the Public Schools, Lafayette, Indiana, October 6–9, 1963; mimeographed), p. 10.

SUGGESTED ACTIVITIES

Written Assignments

1. Some proponents of greater separation of church and state have advocated the abolition of tax exemptions. They argue that tax exemption for churches constitutes "an establishment of religion." Other proponents of greater separation have defended exemptions. They say that taxing religion would be "prohibiting the free exercise thereof."

   a. Is it possible for those agreeing on goals to be opposed on the means to achieve these goals? Why? Why not?

   This assignment grows out of a primary objective of this lesson: To develop tolerance for ambiguity in answering questions of "establishment" and "separation." The First Amendment reads, "Congress shall make no law respecting an establishment of religion or prohibiting the free exercise thereof . . . " Application of this injunction to questions of taxation of church wealth presents a dilemma.

   For some Americans taxing the church would imply "prohibiting the free exercise" of religion. Indeed, _excessive_ taxation would do so. And the observation that "the power to tax is the power to destroy" would be pertinent. Church and state would not then be separate; rather, the state could extinguish the church.

   For other Americans this tax exemption implies a subsidy of the churches "an establishment of religion." Exemption beyond reasonable limits would be establishment, and the observation that the power to exempt is the power to control would be pertinent. Church and state would not be separate; rather, the church would be obligated to the state.

   The crucial question is, "At what point does the degree of taxation bring 'prohibiting,' or conversely, at what point does the degree of exemption bring 'establishment'?" Students should understand the inadequacy of pat answers to this question. Americans, including jurists, clergymen, and laymen, are presently searching for the best answer. Their thoughtful discussion can help.

   b. According to the First Amendment, what should be the government's relation to religion?

   Theoretically, the government's position is one of neutrality. In reality, it is one of _friendly_ neutrality.

   c. Will the answer to (b) help us answer (a)? Why?

   The key to the exemption issue—and to the larger issue of church-state separation—lies in the concept of government neutrality regarding religion. If there were no call for neutrality—if the government were openly hostile or openly supportive—there would be no issue.

2. Some critics of exemptions have said that the churches, by accepting tax exemptions, may endanger themselves. Two specific dangers are noted:

   a. The churches, though gaining financially, face the danger of a _quid pro quo_ situation.

   b. The churches, though gaining financially, are losing spiritually.

Are these dangers real? If you believe that they are, write an essay explaining the exact nature of the danger. Find examples or develop hypothetical situations which support and illustrate your argument. If you do not believe one or both of these are real dangers, explain why they only seem to be.

In this essay students have the opportunity to draw their own conclusions about dangerous consequences to the churches which might result from their tax exempt status. Some points to consider are:

1) maintaining the churches' independent voice and freedom of action; maintaining of their role as an objective judge of society; and, maintaining their undiluted loyalty to their basic spiritual insights.

2) being concerned with spiritual rather than material things; being concerned with righteousness rather than respectability; being concerned with what is ethical rather than with what is legal; and being concerned with the church as a spiritual fellowship rather than with the church as a civil institution.

Just as church leaders disagree on the reality of dangers to the churches, so may students. A variety of conclusions may be drawn based on available evidence and one's own value orientation. Thus, in evaluating the essays emphasis should be placed upon <u>how well</u> students have developed their conclusions, not upon <u>what</u> they have concluded.

Suggestions for Further Research

These areas of investigation are suggested for those students wishing to do additional research. In guiding students in their individual efforts, be sure to use the "Basic Library" as well as the Resource Guide below.

1. In addition to tax exemption, what other privileges or special treatment do churches and clergy enjoy?

2. What other church-state problems have arisen in American history?

3. Make an appointment with your county tax assessor to determine:

   a. what percentage of property in the county is tax-exempt;
   b. what percentage of this total is held by churches;
   c. what the approximate value of this church-held property is; and,
   d. whether all property owned by the churches is directly related to educational, charitable or religious work.

4. What can you learn of the tax policy related to church property and church income in:

   (a) Canada
   (b) Mexico
   (c) France

VOCABULARY

abrogation	corporate	extricating	opulent	sanction
admonition	demeaning	fatuous	philanthropy	seditiously
ambiguous	dilution	forebearance	proscribe	servility
animosity	edifice	fraternal	prudence	subsidy
appease	eleemosynary	freeholder	quid pro quo	unalienable
commonwealth	exempt	indolence	remonstrance	

RESOURCE GUIDE FOR STUDY 4

I. Audio Visual Aids

A. Films

The Bill of Rights of the United States. 20 min., b&w, $4.65
   Encyclopedia Britannica Films, 425 N. Michigan Ave., Chicago, Ill., 60611
This film relates the story of the long struggle for human freedom which led to the creation of the Bill of Rights. It would be used best at the beginning of the study joined with the Henry and Madison readings.

CBS Report: "The Business of Religion." 61 min., b&w
   CBS/Holt Group, 383 Madison Ave., New York, N.Y., 10017
This film presents an excellent and comprehensive survey of the tax exemption issue. The CBS news staff reveals the scope and magnitude of church holdings. Included are interviews with tax officials and church leaders. The film is highly recommended. It would best be used as a supplement to Sections II and III of this study.

This is Our Heritage. 22 min., color.
   Free loan from Religious Heritage of America, 636 Woodward Building, Washington, D.C.
This film looks at the question of religious freedom in the founding of the country. The Bill of Rights is used as a point of reference. The film might be used at the start of the study in conjunction with the Henry and Madison readings.

II. Articles

"Are Churches Fudging on Tax Exemptions?" Christian Century, vol. 84 (April 5, 1967).

"Congress Shall Make No Law . . . " Saturday Review, vol. 50 (January 21, 1967, February 18, 1967, and March 18, 1967).

"Federal Aid and Judicial Review," Christian Century, vol. 82 (April 14, 1965).

"God is Rich," Harpers, vol. 235 (October, 1967).

"High Price Paid for Tax Status," Christian Century, vol. 79 (April 14, 1965).

"Religion and the Constitution," Christian Century, vol. 82 (February 10, 1965).

"Rendering Unto Caesar," Christian Century, vol. 84 (October 4, 1967).

"Should Church Assets and Income be Taxed?" Christian Century, vol. 85 (July 17, 1968).

"Should Churches be Allowed to do Business Tax-Free?" Reader's Digest, volume 94 (March, 1969).

"Should Church Property be Taxed?" U.S. News and World Report, volume 63 (July 10, 1967).

"Should Churches be Exempt from Business Taxes?" Reader's Digest, volume 79 (November, 1961).

"Should Churches be Taxed?" Congress Biweekly (American Jewish Congress), volume 36 (March 24, 1969).

"Tax the Churches Too?" Christian Century, volume 84 (March 29, 1967).

"Textbooks and the Taxpayer, Future of the First Amendment," America, volume 119 (July 9, 1968).

"Two Walls Not One: Separation Between Church and State," America, volume 117 (December 2, 1967).

"Winery Pays its Back Taxes," Christian Century, volume 78 (December 20, 1961).

III. Books

Gordis, Robert. The Root and the Branch: Judaism and the Free Society. Chicago: University of Chicago Press. $3.95

Pfeffer, Leo. Church, State and Freedom. Revised edition. Boston: Beacon Press. $15.00

Robertson, D. B. Should Churches Be Taxed? Philadelphia: Westminster Press. $6.50

Wolf, Donald J., S.J. Toward Consensus: Catholic-Protestant Interpretations of Church and State. Garden City, New York: Doubleday Anchorbook (paper) $1.45

(In the Basic Library, particular attention is called to the following volumes:

Mead, The Lively Experiment

Stedman, Religion & Politics in America

Stokes and Pfeffer, Church and State in the United States

Wilson, Church and State in American History)

5

THE CHURCHES ON THE AMERICAN FRONTIER

THE PLAN OF THE STUDY

Introduction

The Churches and the Frontier

Religious Influences on the Frontier

Colleges and Universities on the Frontier

Town Meeting on the Frontier

Contemporary Parallel

Suggested Activities

Vocabulary

Resource Guide

THE FOCUS FOR THIS STUDY

This Study focuses upon migration and the part that religion played on the American frontier. Migration is broadly defined as a permanent or semipermanent change in residence, which involves movement between communities. For each migrant the change involves an origin, a destination, and intervening obstacles, one of which is the distance of the migration. History shows the influence on many factors in decisions to migrate: political oppression, religious persecution, the threat of starvation, a sense of adventure, an urge to improve one's material lot in life, an urge to alter one's life style, a desire to join relatives, etc. These reasons, "push" and "pull" factors, must be supplemented by considering the migrant's mental state—his perception of two environments, the one where he is and the one which is a possible alternative. America was such a possible alternative to many Europeans and many came to the "new world." The American frontier was such an alternative to persons living in the Eastern United States, and many choose to migrate.

Uprooting one's self and family to journey to a new area and make a new home is a difficult and demanding task, even for migrants who are forced to move. The adjustments are psychological, as well as geographic and economic, and the stress of movement is great as migrants separate themselves from the community of origin and seek to gain acceptance and a sense of "belonging" in the new community. The migrants to the frontier often sought to ease the difficulties of adjustment by making the new community similar to the desirable qualities of his "old" community. Thus, many migrants established churches and synagogues, and through these organizations improved human conditions on the frontier.

While the frontier is closed today, scholars and reporters still write of the uprooted feeling of Americans, and their great migration from place to place: country to city, city to city. These twentieth century migrants still seek acceptance and a sense of belonging in communities. They search for meaning in their lives and for satisfaction. What is the role of religion in this mobile society? The "contemporary parallel" section of this Study poses this question for students once they have examined religion on the Western frontier.

THE OBJECTIVES FOR THIS STUDY

Knowledge Objectives—Each student will demonstrate his knowledge that:

1. The religions of America accompanied in varying degrees the Western settler, and thus, influenced the social and economic development of the migrants and their communities.

2. The religions played a number of roles on the frontier in addition to spreading their religious traditions: notably, education, peace-making, and "civilizing" the frontier.

3. Both Western-born and established Eastern churches organized and directed religious activity on the frontier.

4. Church organization made important contributions to the development of higher education in America.

5. Religion may influence the social and economic development of a people.

Skill Objectives—Each student will demonstrate his ability to:

1. Analyze maps for information relative to answering sets of questions.

2. Draw inferences from data presented on maps.

3. Make comparisons among data presented on maps and to generalize using that data.

4. Make generalizations concerning the relationship of religion to developing social environment on the American frontier.

Attitude and Value Objectives—Each student will demonstrate his willingness to:

1. Participate in class discussion, using the data on maps in order to generalize about the relationships between religious organizations and westward migration in the United States.

2. Support judgments and conclusions with reference to evidence and reasons open to class evaluation through discussion, without "unloading" with unsupported assertions.

3. Prepare the paper (or participate in the discussion) accompanying the "Town Meeting on the Frontier" section.

INTRODUCTION

The first part of this study is designed to have students gain information about the expansion of the churches on the frontier. From the East, church bodies sent preachers, money and supplies to meet the spiritual needs of the settlers. Where and to what extent they were successful can be revealed in some measure by maps. The maps used in this lesson present a survey of the number of churches in each county. From them one can determine where a particular body is found and approximately in what strength. Patterns of expansion are also revealed. Some knowledge of the relative strength of the denominations can be derived from these maps. Finally, by comparing these "expansion" maps with a topographical map, one may see the influence of natural conditions upon patterns of expansion.

Beyond gaining knowledge of church expansion on the frontier, a principal purpose of this exercise is to have students gain knowledge in the use of maps. Thus time should be spent discussing what kinds of information a map can and cannot provide. In the case at hand, neither the types of religious activities nor the reasons for such activities are indicated by maps. The teacher of social studies must help students learn what kinds of information are better conveyed visually than verbally and how such information is symbolically represented. General questions are provided in the student materials to direct students to the significant data on the maps. Specific questions for each map are designed to have students gain special information about a church body.

THE CHURCHES AND THE FRONTIER

It is suggested that this section be handled as a teacher-led-discussion. Most questions in the student materials can be answered by referring to the maps; however, some must be fully answered by the teacher. The following information is offered to help in answering questions in the student material. Teachers may wish to elaborate and even develop a lecture-discussion session based on the maps.

Baptist Churches in 1850

1. In what parts of the country are the greatest concentrations of Baptist churches found?

In New England, New York, the southern states—North and South Carolina, Georgia, Alabama, Tennessee, and Kentucky.

2. From New York south, are the Baptists generally more prominent in coastal or interior regions? In rural areas or around cities? (Check a map showing cities.)

Baptists were found in the interior and rural areas. The coastal, tidewater regions had been preempted by earlier settlers.

3. By 1850 where had Baptists crossed the Mississippi River in significant numbers?

The Baptists crossed the Mississippi and settled, most notably, just north of St. Louis, Missouri. They also located in southern Arkansas and Louisiana.

4. What might account for the heavy settlement of Baptists along the South Carolina-Georgia border?

The Savannah River, which flows down to the port city of Savannah.

Congregational Churches in 1850

1. In 1850 most Congregational Churches were found in what seven states?

Congregationalists were found primarily in the New England states (Maine, New Hampshire, Vermont, Massachusetts, Rhode Island, Connecticut), plus New York.

2. From its New England origin, in what direction did Congregationalism expand?

They moved westerly, with virtually no penetration to the south.

3. How might the one South Carolina congregation have traveled from Massachusetts? (It did so at the end of the seventeenth century.)

Coastal travel by ship, especially in the seventeenth century, was far simpler than overland journeys. No post roads were to be found this early in American history.

Episcopal Churches in 1850

1. The Episcopal Church was the official or established church of the southern colonies. By 1850 is there still evidence of their early favored position? If so, where?

Evidence of previous "establishment" of the Church of England prior to the Revolution is found in Maryland, South Carolina, and Virginia.

2. Where are the major settlements along the Mississippi River? What cities are here?

Major settlements were found at St. Louis, Memphis, and New Orleans.

3. Judging from this map, how successful was the Episcopal Church on the frontier?

The Episcopal Church made only limited ventures into frontier areas, particularly in the Old Northwest.

Lutheran Churches in 1850

1. Judging from the map, at what port (the major ones were Boston, New York, Philadelphia and Charleston) did most settlers of the great eighteenth century Lutheran migrations land?

Philadelphia, as should be evident from the great concentration in Pennsylvania, was the major port of entry for Lutheran immigrants.

2. From that port city, in what direction did the (German) Lutheran churches move?

They moved due west in great numbers, but also southwesterly along the Blue Ridge Mountains.

3. What might account for the line of churches south from the "panhandle" of Maryland through Virginia?

These valleys (e.g., the Shenandoah) and mountain ridges were a natural migration path into the South. Also, land here was still available, unlike the great plantation areas to the east.

4. Where might Lutherans coming from Europe have entered the Deep South?

Lutherans who settled in South Carolina probably landed at Charleston or, in some cases, Savannah, Georgia.

Methodist Churches in 1850

1. Though Methodism arrived "late" in America, that is, in the Revolutionary Period itself, it was quite strong by 1850. In what states bordering the Atlantic was this true?

<u>Methodists were quite strong in Maine, Massachusetts, Rhode Island, Connecticut, New York, New Jersey, Maryland, and South Carolina.</u>

2. Locate the Ohio River. Could you defend the statement that "this was a highway of migration for the Methodists"?

<u>The Ohio River extends from Pennsylvania's western border to its conjunction with the Mississippi River at the southern tip of Illinois. It is obviously a major route into the western interior.</u>

3. Compared with maps you have already seen (for example, that of the Congregational Churches), what does this one tell us about the strength of Methodism on the frontier?

<u>Clearly the Methodists, like the Baptists, are by 1850 making great inroads along the frontier, keeping pace with the rapid settlement of newly opened territories. (You might reshow the Baptist</u> map here comparing it and the Methodist map with some of the groups who were less numerous or less successful on the frontier.)

Presbyterian Churches in 1850

1. Presbyterians did not arrive in great numbers in America until the eighteenth century. From looking at this map, what evidence do you find that they located uncrowded and cheaper land farther west?

<u>The most striking evidence is in western Pennsylvania. But also see Kentucky, Tennessee, and Ohio.</u>

2. Using a topographical map, trace the migration from central Pennsylvania through Virginia to eastern Tennessee. What effect might topography have on settlement and thus the establishment of churches?

Have the students study a topographic map, either a wall map or one at their desks. Then have them follow the valleys and ridges that flow in a southwesterly direction from central Pennsylvania. What looks like uneven or irregular patterns of church expansion are often to be partly explained in terms of <u>impassable mountain ranges, inviting valleys, navigable rivers and the like.</u>

3. Presbyterians and Congregationalists cooperated in much of their "home mission" effort to win the West. Compare the 1850 maps of these two groups. Which group was more successful? What might be an explanation for this?

<u>The Plan of Union, adopted in 1801, represents this joint Congregational-Presbyterian effort. It resulted in the founding of such colleges as Grinnell, Beloit, and Knox. The Presbyterians had an edge in at least two ways in this common drive. One, they maintained closer ties with newly founded churches through their presbytery and synod structure; Congregationalism lacked such a structure. Second, when the westward push began in earnest, the Presbyterians already had a greater geographical spread (from Long Island to Georgia) than did the Congregationalists, who were so heavily concentrated in the Northeast.</u>

Quaker Churches (Meetings) in 1850

1. While Quakers did not ever become a large group in America, they were a quite important group in the early history of the country. What is sometimes called the "Quaker State"? Why?

Pennsylvania, founded in 1681 by William Penn, was first settled by Quakers from southern England. Though they soon lost a numerical superiority, the Quakers remained strong in the Philadelphia area as the map shows.

2. Locate Rhode Island on the map. What aspects of this colony's early history could help account for the Quaker concentration there?

Under Roger Williams, Rhode Island promised a "full liberty in religious concernments." Steadily harassed and persecuted most everywhere else in the colonial period (except, of course, Pennsylvania), Quakers settled in large numbers in Rhode Island.

3. Some important Quaker colleges today are Haverford and Swarthmore (in Pennsylvania), Guilford (North Carolina), and Earlham (Indiana). From looking at this map, where in the states indicated would these schools probably be found?

Both Haverford and Swarthmore are in the greater Philadelphia area. Guilford is in north central North Carolina, and Earlham is in eastern Indiana.

Roman Catholic Churches in 1850

1. One of the thirteen colonies was founded by Roman Catholics from England. From looking at this map can you tell which colony it was?

Maryland, founded by Lord Baltimore in 1632, continued to be a Catholic stronghold. The city of Baltimore became in 1789 the first diocesan center in America under Bishop John Carroll.

2. The eastern half of Canada was French and Catholic. What evidence can you see of the influence of Canadian Catholicism in the United States?

Note especially the northern tip of Maine, upstate New York, and northern Michigan.

3. In the eighteenth century, French Catholics were quite active in the Mississippi Valley. What signs of this can be seen?

The French worked the Mississippi from both ends. They moved up the St. Lawrence through and around the Great Lakes to the upper reaches of the valley. (Recall Father Marquette's exploration of the river along with Louis Joliet in 1673.) In 1718 the French founded New Orleans, which became a major center of mission activity, especially through the Jesuit Order (Society of Jesus).

4. Alone among America's major religious groups in 1850, the Roman Catholics had significant church strength west of the Mississippi River? What might account for this?

Catholic strength in the West relates, of course, to Spain's (later Mexico's) control of this area down to the Mexican-American War in 1846-47. Notable is the major center in Santa Fe (Holy Faith), New Mexico, founded in 1610. Also, the famous chain of missions in California founded by the Franciscan Junipero Serra should be mentioned. The earliest of these missions was established in San Diego in 1769; the last one in Ventura (San Buenaventura) in 1782.

New Churches in the American West

(Note: As these churches arose on the frontier in the mid-nineteenth century, no 1850 maps are provided. However, any political map of the U.S. may be used regarding the Disciples and a 1950 map is provided showing Mormon strength.)

1. You may simply indicate on a wall map the area of Disciple strength in 1850. The point to be emphasized is how much this church is itself a product of the West and of the frontier.

2. If any church in America today deserves to be called western, it is the Church of Jesus Christ of Latter-day Saints, with headquarters not in Boston, New York or Philadelphia, but Salt Lake City, Utah. Questions may arise about Smith's murder, and this could be an occasion for individual research into Mormon history. Non-Mormons persecuted and abused the Mormon community on many grounds, of which the charges regarding polygamy were only one.

Expansion in and around Utah was made possible by the fact that the Mormons were the only strong, centrally organized religious group in that region. The church had good discipline and excellent organization.

Judaism on the Frontier

Students might begin by plotting the frontier synagogues: Louisville, New Orleans, St. Louis, Cleveland, and Cincinnati. With these locations in mind, turn to the reading and the accompanying questions.

1. Why, even in the West, did Jews tend to prefer the city to the farm?

The Jewish immigrants at this time came from an urban experience in Europe. Adjusting to a new land was difficult, and the Jewish migrants sought a more familiar urban environment where they could practice their faith together.

2. What is meant by the phrase "hemmed in by medieval restrictions"?

These medieval restrictions were limitations on the rights to travel, own land, freedom of residence, freedom of occupation, freedom of education, and of religious expression.

3. Would the American frontier be likely to have "discriminatory regulations"? Why or why not?

Students are asked here to draw inferences from their study of life on the American frontier. Teachers should ask for student judgments and request a justificatory argument for their judgments. Close attention should be paid to the reasons students offer and the evidence backing their judgments.

Students interested in the Jewish migrants might read into the paperback by Bertram W. Korn, cited in the Study, or the three volume work by Jacob R. Marcus, Memoirs of American Jews, 1776-1865 (Philadelphia: The Jewish Publication Society of America, 1954-5).

RELIGIOUS INFLUENCES ON THE FRONTIER

Upon completion of the discussion of the maps, students should read these four "testimonies." While the maps illustrate the extent of church activity on the frontier, these readings illuminate the nature of that activity. Each reading presents a somewhat different "slant" on frontier religion. Initially, we are told what will happen on the frontier vis-a-vis religion, then what is happening, and finally what has happened. Since each reading is rather straightforward, no guiding questions are needed. However, at the end of each reading, questions to serve as the bases of discussion are provided. Thus the nature of religious activity is to be explored in a teacher-led discussion. Also, it must be noted that answers to these questions cannot be fully drawn from the student readings. The following material can be used in answering those questions and expanding upon the readings.

Lyman Beecher

1. When Beecher speaks of the East aiding the West, does this give you some hint of to whom the Plea is directed?

Home mission boards and other agencies in such cities as Boston, New York, and Philadelphia looked after their own members as they traveled west. They also sought to build churches or establish schools wherever the population was sufficient to justify it.

2. What does Beecher think will happen to the West if religion does not keep up with the advancing frontier?

Immorality and illiteracy will prevail, in Beecher's view, wherever "Heaven's instruments" are not found.

3. What sort of aid might he seek?

Aid was primarily in three forms: a) trained personnel: teachers and preachers, b) money for salaries or buildings, c) literature: tracts, books, periodicals, Bibles.

John Mason Peck

1. What interest does this missionary have in education? Why?

Peck, who also founded schools and colleges, obviously had a strong interest in promoting learning and in seeing that the "right sort" of literature was available. In Christianity, as in Judaism, the tie with education and learning has always been close—on the assumption that God is to be served with the whole mind, too.

2. Why did people hear preaching only once a month?

The critical shortage of clergy on the frontier meant either that the minister had to travel in a wide circuit from week to week, or that the people had to make a long journey—perhaps 2 or 3 days—to a town that had a church and a settled preacher. (Note the route the books would take: from Boston south to New Orleans, then north to St. Louis. The reason, obviously, for this roundabout way is that water travel was so much easier and cheaper than land travel.)

Peter Cartwright

1. What other attraction, besides religion, might bring several hundred people of the frontier together for a four or five day camp-meeting?

Certainly, social needs were met in the camp meetings as they were seldom met elsewhere on the frontier. Young people had a chance to meet each other, older people a chance to talk about common problems, children to play with large numbers of other children.

Education was another need met by these meetings, though the usual caricature of the camp meeting is that only shouting and fainting went on. In the long ("protracted") meeting, religious instruction was a regular feature. For younger children, it could provide their first systematic instruction in how to read and write.

2. On the basis of Cartwright's testimony, how successful were revivals and camp meetings in making new converts?

Cartwright is, of course, an enthusiastic supporter of revivals and is to that extent, therefore, an interested witness. However, revivalism was clearly a most successful instrument for recruitment, especially among Baptists, Methodists, Presbyterians, and Disciples of Christ. It was less successful among the other groups considered earlier in this lesson.

Pierre Jean DeSmet, S.J.

1. On the basis of General Stanley's letter, what could you conclude about the relationship between the Indians and at least some missionaries?

From the colonial period through the nineteenth and even into the twentieth centuries, many missionaries came to be trusted by Indians who saw in so many other white men only betrayal or deceit. The missionary record is not a perfect one, of course, but on the whole the relationship between them and the tribes they served was one of mutual respect and genuine humane concern.

2. Also judging from the letter, what larger role in American history do you see some of the frontier priests or preachers having?

Missionaries on the frontier often were the only ones who knew conditions or people well enough to be of help to those back East—including the U.S. Government. Priests and preachers served as guides (John Mason Peck even wrote a guide for emigrants to Illinois), teachers, physicians, Indian agents, and—as we have seen in the case of Father DeSmet—peacemakers. One Presbyterian missionary to the West, Sheldon Jackson, later served in Alaska where he saved the Eskimos from the threat of starvation by introducing reindeer from nearby Siberia. So the image of the frontier preacher must be enlarged to make room for these varied and valuable services. Consequently, the role of the churches in civilizing the frontier must also be seen in broader terms than it normally is.

COLLEGES AND UNIVERSITIES ON THE FRONTIER

In the development of the West, the major denominational bodies contributed greatly through the establishment of colleges and universities. While some later foundered, many of these colleges have become major seats of learning in the U.S. In the burgeoning frontier settlements they provided teachers, preachers, doctors and lawyers.

The basic sources of information in this section are a list of colleges and an outline map.

1. Select those colleges founded between 1820 and 1830 and find their location on the map provided.

   a. Where are most of these colleges located?

   b. How many are west of the Mississippi River?

   c. Who is establishing these colleges? Governmental or denominational agencies?

   The establishment of colleges followed closely the patterns of settlement. Along the paths of migration and into the most favored territories colleges were founded. The old Northwest was an early goal of settlers, and this is reflected in the number of institutions established there. Especially active in the 1820-1830 decade were Baptists, Congregationalists, and Presbyterians.

2. Now find the location of those founded between 1840 and 1850.

   a. Where were most of the colleges established at this time?

   b. How many in this period are west of the Mississippi River?

   c. Which denominations are most active?

   In the 1840-1850 decade the old Northwest continues to witness the birth of new colleges. However, college founding has now spread northwest and southwest across the Mississippi River. During this period the Methodists are particularly active in establishing colleges. (Note also German Reformed and United Brethren churches not previously mentioned.)

3. After plotting these colleges on the map, what generalizations could you make about the educational role of the churches compared to that of the state?

   Before 1850 the churches of America far outshone the states in providing institutions of higher learning. In the 1820-1830 decade, the ratio is 11 to 1; in the 1840-1850 period the ratio on the frontier is 33 to 1!

You will need to supply students with an outline map so they may plot the locations of colleges. Or, you could use a slated (blackboard) map and lead a total group activity.

TOWN MEETING ON THE FRONTIER

In the town meeting the full variety of motives supporting or rejecting the church can be brought out. The banker and storekeeper, for example, may have far different reasons for welcoming the church than do housewives and mothers. Some frontier dwellers profited from lawlessness, Indian wars, and "the freedom" from religiously sanctioned social constraints.

This activity may be undertaken by individual students as a written assignment. However, an alternate suggestion is to have a group of able students simulate an 1850 frontier town meeting for presentation to the class. While students are encouraged to use their imaginations in either case, what is probable should be stressed.

CONTEMPORARY PARALLEL

This study emphasizes the expansion of the churches along the American frontier and the influence that they had in those difficult days. Today the institutional church (the major denominations) is not expanding; it is declining in membership, attendance, and perceived influence. The process of secularization has presented a crisis for the churches. This contemporary parallel presents some of the issues involved in the modern predicament facing the church.

The total recorded membership of all religious bodies listed in the 1970 Yearbook of American Churches was 63.1 percent of the U.S. population in 1969. Comparable membership figures reported in the 1971 Yearbook represented 62.4 percent of the U.S. population in 1970. Thus the percentage of church membership has taken a downward trend. Far more significant than membership statistics, however, are those that reveal actual attendance. Students should study the following tables and offer their interpretations of the data. What is the significance in the gradual decline in church participation? Even more important, what is the explanation of the fact that Americans perceive that religion is losing its influence? Why are younger people and the educated more likely to feel that religion is losing its influence?

TABLE 1

PERCENTAGE OF AMERICANS ATTENDING CHURCH DURING
AN AVERAGE WEEK, 1955–66

Year	Percentage
1955	49%
1956	46%
1957	47%
1958	49%
1959	47%
1960	47%
1961	47%
1962	46%
1963	46%
1964	45%
1965	44%
1966	44%

Source: George Gallup Poll as quoted in Information Service, Volume XLVI, Number 2, January 28, 1967.

TABLE 2

AMERICANS FEEL RELIGION IS LOSING ITS INFLUENCE

At the present time, do you think religion as a whole is increasing its influence on American life, or losing its influence?

	1957	1962	1965	1967
INCREASING	69%	45%	33%	23%
LOSING	14	31	45	57
NO DIFFERENCE	10	17	13	14
NO OPINION	7	7	9	6

Source: George Gallup Poll as quoted in The Cleveland Press, April 18, 1967.

TABLE 3

YOUNGER PEOPLE AND THE EDUCATED ARE MORE LIKELY
TO FEEL THAT RELIGION IS LOSING ITS INFLUENCE

PERCENTAGE SAYING RELIGION IS LOSING ITS INFLUENCE, 1967

AGE:

21–29 years	63%
30–49 years	57%
50 and over	53%

EDUCATION:

College	60%
High School	59%
Grade School	52%

Source: George Gallup Poll as quoted in The Cleveland Press, April 18, 1967.

One of the most provocative ways of looking at the above data is suggested by Dietrich Bonhoeffer's famous words written from prison on April 30, 1944: "We are proceeding toward a time of no religion at all. . . . How do we speak of God without religion. . . . How do we speak in a secular fashion of God?" Harvey Cox, American theologian and author of the influential book, The Secular City, argues that modern secular (from saeculum = "this present age") man turns his attention away from worlds beyond and toward this world and this time. What might this observation suggest about the decline in church attendance?

Cox also addresses himself to Bonhoeffer's question, "How do we speak in a secular fashion of God?" He writes:

> Speaking of God in a secular fashion . . . entails our discerning where God is working and then joining His work. Standing in a picket line is a way of speaking. By doing it a Christian speaks of God. He helps alter the word "God: by changing the society in which it has been trivialized, by moving away from the context where "God-talk" usually occurs, and by shedding the stereotyped roles in which God's name is usually intoned."[1]

Does this interpretation help to explain what is happening to institutional religion today? What is implied by "moving away from the context where 'God-talk' usually occurs"? What other ways than standing in a picket line might portray speaking in a secular fashion of God? Are religious "happenings" occurring outside the four walls of the church? Where? What are the frontiers of the church today?

SUGGESTED ACTIVITIES

It is suggested that each student be given the opportunity to choose one of the activities as his written assignment for this lesson.

An Account in a New York Newspaper

As a reporter for a paper you have spent four months on the frontier. You were astonished by the vast difference between frontier life and life "back East." The places you visited were not influenced by any church or missionary.

If the churches had played no role on the frontier, what difference would this have made? As the newspaper reporter in 1850, comment on the way (you feel) people might have ordered their lives—their livelihoods, their relationships with others, their leisure time and their family life.

This should be the least difficult assignment and could be suggested to less able students. Some things to be considered here are manners and morals, respect for the law, education, cooperation among settlers, wholesome social activities centered around the church, as well as purely religious activities.

A Speech to Potential Supporters

As a missionary to the western frontier you have returned to Boston to raise funds for the mission effort. In a speech you are to deliver to the governing board of a large church body, you wish to convince your audience—mostly businessmen—of the wisdom of supporting church activity on the frontier. You decide to describe the different types of "returns" that can be expected from their "investment."

In this speech students should touch on the variety of "returns" society might reap from church activity on the frontier. Material prosperity depends in great part upon an ordered society. The chaos and lawlessness of some areas hindered development. Education was necessary for progress, also. The level of living of frontier people rose with increased education. New industries and the demand for eastern products accompanied the rise in educational level. Rights of private property must be respected along with human rights for successful democracy. The resources of the West could contribute greatly to the prosperity of the East. New markets in the West were also ready for development

---

[1] Harvey Cox, The Secular City (New York: The Macmillan Company, 1965), pp. 256–257.

The frontier had to be tamed, though, before its potential could be realized. The churches contribute to that taming process.

Of course, there are other (perhaps better) reasons than the above materialistic ones for sending missionaries to the West. In this exercise, however, the "investment return" metaphor is emphasized.

Suggestions for Further Research

These areas of investigation are suggested for those students wishing to do additional research. In guiding students in their individual efforts, be sure to use the "Basic Library" as well as the Resource Guide below.

1. Investigate the mission efforts among the Indians at the present time.

2. How many church-related colleges are in your state? When were they founded, and by what religious group?

3. The newest frontiers for Americans are Alaska and Hawaii. What can you learn about the religious development in each of these states?

VOCABULARY

adversaries	illiteracy	remuneration	testimony
concur	migration	spiritual	topographic
consecrated	mock	temporal	tract
formidable			

RESOURCE GUIDE FOR STUDY 5

I. Audio Visual Aids

A. Films

Alaskan Discovery. 30 min., color, Rental $12.00
　　The American Lutheran Church, 426 S. Fifth St., Minneapolis, Minn. (or Cathedral Films, 2921 W. Alameda Ave., Burbank, Calif.)
A missionary and Eskimo layman offer their views of contemporary Alaska and the 49th state. Photographically beautiful.

Altars of God. 15 min., b&w, Rental $3.00
　　Presbyterian Distribution Service, 475 Riverside Dr., New York, N.Y. 10027
Through a personally-conducted tour of a "Cattlemen's campmeeting," we gain a glimpse of the religious life of western rural American families. The church wagon, prayer tree, and big-top meeting are described as well as some of the problems, hopes, and dreams of the people involved. Shown here is the modern frontier.

Frontier in the West. 21 min., color, Rental $8.00
　　Southern Baptist Convention, 127 Ninth Ave., Nashville, Tenn.
An example of one denomination, the Southern Baptist Convention, meeting spiritual needs on the western frontier.

Heritage to Destiny. 30 min., Rental $7.00
    Available from Disciples of Christ (United Christian Missionary Society) 222 S. Downey Avenue, Indianapolis, Indiana 46207
This film depicts the history of the Disciples of Christ Church from its birth on the Western frontier.

Oregon Trail. 25 min., b&w, Rental $5.65
    Encyclopedia Britannica Films, 425 N. Michigan Ave., Chicago, Ill. 60611
This film dramatizes the experiences of a pioneer family migrating to Oregon in a wagon train; shows how they are involved not only in the forces of history, but also with their own human family problems. Stressing the difficulties and hardships of the journey, the film highlights the long treks under the burning prairie sun, the dangerous river crossings, the threat of an Indian attack, the climb through the mountains and the arrival in the Willamette Valley in Oregon.

Pioneer Community of the Midwest. 14 min., color, Rental $4.75
    Coronet Films, 65 E. South Water St., Chicago, Illinois 60601
Explains that the trails and waterways by which the pioneers travelled to the Midwest influenced the location of pioneer towns. Shows the blacksmith and shoemaker's shops, water-driven flour and lumber mills, and describes the roles of the pioneer doctor, schoolmaster, itinerant preacher, and circuit court judge. The film depicts life in those areas treated in the map activities in this study.

Real West. 54 min., b&w, $10.75
    McGraw-Hill (Text-film dept.), 330 W. 42nd St., New York, N.Y. 10009
An authentic panoramic view of America's frontier days . . . the American West (1849–1900) as it really was when the pioneers moved westward to fill the last frontier. Winner of the Prix Italia Grand Prize as the best television documentary. Although this film concerns the trans-Mississippi West, it shows the type of existence common to most frontier areas.

B. Filmstrips

Hawaii and Missions. color, sale $6.00
    United Church of Christ, 1501 Race St., Philadelphia, Pennsylvania.
A survey of Hawaiian history through statehood, with emphasis on the influence of Christian missions.

II. Articles

"Bright Vignettes of a Lost World; Journals of Nicholas Point," Life, volume 63 (December 1, 1967).
    Story of French Jesuit, Nicholas Point, and his evangelizing and living among the Flatheads, Coeur d' Alenes and Blackfeet Indians in 1835.

"Farewell to Shannon Brown," Sports Illustrated, volume 14 (April 3, 1961).
    Story of how sports at a mission in Wyoming helped the Indians. Especially interesting to boys.

"Marquette League Jubilee: Catholic Indian Missions," America, volume 91 (September 18, 1954).

"Murder at the Place of Rye Grass," American Heritage, volume 10 (August 1959).
    Story of Narcissa and Marcus Whitman.

"White Father is Heap Bad Medicine: Monsignor Stadtmuller Thrown Off the Reservation in Isleta, New Mexico," Life, volume 59 (July 16, 1965).
This article gives an interesting insight into some problems today concerning the church and the Indians.

III. Books

Beaver, R. Pierce. Church, State and the American Indians. St. Louis: Concordia. $6.75

Daughtery, James. Marcus and Narcissa Whitman: Pioneers of Oregon. New York: Viking. $3.95

Judd, Gerrit P. Hawaii: An Informal History. New York: Macmillan Collier. (paper) $.95

LaFarge, Oliver. The American Indian. New York: Golden Press. $5.95

Lineberry, William P. New States: Alaska and Hawaii. New York: Wilson. $3.50

Spring, Norma. Alaska: Pioneer State. Camden, New Jersey: Nelson. $4.50

Terrell, John U. Black Robe: The Life of Pierre-Jean DeSmet. Garden City, New York: Doubleday (Dolphin) (paper) $4.95

Tewksbury, Donald G. The Founding of American Colleges and Universities Before the Civil War. Hamden, Connecticut: Shoe String Press. $6.00

Veglahn, Nancy. Peter Cartwright: Pioneer Circuit Rider. New York: Scribner. $3.95

(In the Basic Library, particular attention is called to the following volumes:

    Gaustad, Historical Atlas of Religion in America, Parts II, IV

    Hudson, Religion in America

    Niebuhr, The Social Sources of Denominationalism)

6

BLACKS AND THE CHURCHES

THE PLAN OF THE STUDY

Introduction

The Church as Refuge and Hope

The Church Divided and Reproached

Christianity Abandoned and Christianity Challenged

Contemporary Parallel

Suggested Activities

Vocabulary

Resource Guide

THE FOCUS OF THIS STUDY

The history of the black man in America is finding its way into the textbooks of the nation's schools and is constantly before the American public through the mass media. This Study focuses upon an important part of that history—the place of Christianity and the black church from the antebellum period to our era with the impassioned appeals of Malcolm X, Martin Luther King, Jr., and other black leaders. In this study, students have an opportunity to analyze and reflect upon various source materials from the early nineteenth century through the 1960's. In the contemporary parallel section, the students can conduct independent or group research on issues involving minorities and religion in America. The black experience and religion, and other minorities' experiences and religion, certainly meet most criteria to be labeled "significant" and "important" areas for student inquiry, and would seem to be "relevant" to students' interests and vital to our lives together.

THE OBJECTIVES FOR THIS STUDY

Knowledge Objectives—Each student will demonstrate his knowledge that:

1. Information about Negro religion may be obtained from a study of spirituals, sermons, church documents, and historical commentaries.

2. Black Christianity played an important role in aiding black Americans to survive their period of enslavement, and the black church has served social functions and fulfilled individual needs (spiritual and secular) as the black man faced a social system marked by adversity and anxiety.

3. Emphases in black religion have included preparation for a better life in the next world and, increasingly, a more abundant life in this world.

4. The slavery issue created bitter disputes among the white churches, and divisions which have lasted to today.

5. Negro leaders have differed in their attitudes toward Christianity and its place in Negro life.

Skill Objectives—Each student will demonstrate his ability to:

1. Extract evidence from a variety of historical sources, including Negro spirituals, sermons, and personal accounts.

2. Compare and contrast the positions and arguments of several black leaders on religious issues.

3. Generalize about the place of churches in Negro life, past and present, in terms of their role (functions), the probable causes for the importance of the Black church, and the goals sought.

Attitude and Value Objectives—Each student will demonstrate his willingness to:

1. Evaluate the efforts of religious organizations and black leaders to improve the life style of black Americans, developing criteria for such evaluation based upon personal values which are open for public discussion and are logically consistent.

2. Consider ideas which may be challenging to one's own attitudes and accepted explanations, reflecting upon both newly-received and personal beliefs and their reliability and justification.

3. Show empathy for the black American in the various historical periods noted in the Study, by arguing from a different perspective or by role playing activities.

4. Confront situations a) wherein he must decide what "treating other people as equals" means in terms of behavior and b) wherein he must infer what Christian ideals indicate as responsible conduct for Christians.

INTRODUCTION

On the ante-bellum plantations of the South, a distinctly Afro-American musical form was born. The spiritual was an expression of the unique Christianity of the Negro slave. The Negro believed that even in his state of bondage he was a "child of God." In this belief the slave found the hope, strength, and inspiration necessary to transcend the vicissitudes of life however cruel. This sense of being "created in God's image" provided the genius of the spiritual. The raw material for spirituals is derived from three main sources: the Bible, the world of nature and personal experiences of religion.[1]

It is desirable to obtain recordings of the spirituals (see bibliography for some suggestions), for appreciation of the spiritual as a historical document and as an art work is enhanced if students can hear them sung in their original form. Each spiritual has its own "mood"—joy, sadness, hope, resignation, conviction—which can be conveyed only partially by a reading of the words. Students may note slight word differences between the recordings and the spirituals as presented here. If, however, recordings are unobtainable, you should proceed, utilizing only the words of the spiritual.

---

[1] Howard Thurman, Deep River (Mills College, California: The Eucalyptus Press, 1945).

Without introduction or explanation, present the spirituals to the class. If no recordings are available, have students read through each spiritual. After hearing and reading the spirituals, ask the students to determine what we can learn from an examination of spirituals about the life and religion of the slave. Students may not understand some of the references in the spirituals. Thus you may have to point out, or have a student explain, Biblical references such as Canaan, Jonah, the Hebrew children, or references to nature such as the inch-worms.

Class discussion of the spirituals may center around the questions in the student material:

1. What does each spiritual tell us about the "things that mattered most" to those who created these spirituals?

2. Would this indicate to us some of the conditions of life of the blacks at the time they were written? If so, what conditions?

3. What are the central themes of the spirituals?

4. Would these spirituals also indicate to us the role the church played in lives of the blacks?

In some spirituals Negroes, as God's children, identify with others who suffered adversity but were "delivered" by God. Thus the spiritual may express the hope, even the conviction, that God will soon "deliver" the Negro, too. Much in the Negro spiritual is, of course, open to wide interpretation. For example, "Canaan" may mean a celestial heaven, but it may also mean the free North, or even Africa! The theme of freedom runs through most of the spirituals presented here. Some equate death with freedom while others predict a freedom on this earth. The conviction that bondage and misery will end with God's help is very obvious. Note the similarity of the following lines:

(The Gospel Ship) landed me over on Canaan's shore an' I'll never come back no more.

(Jesus) will help us to the end.
I don't expect to stay much longer here.

I'll be buried in my grave
An' go home to my Lord an' be free.

You may hinder me here but you cannot there,
'Cause God in Heaven goin' to answer prayer.

Didn't come here for to stay always,

I did know my Jesus heard me . . .
An' you, too, shall be free.

The firm belief that one will get to heaven was accompanied by a dogged determination to "bear up" under the cruelties of bondage. The inch-by-inch labored movement of a creature common to the southern woodlands provided an appropriate model for the Negro struggle.

Though the Negro was indoctrinated with the assertion that slavery was sanctioned by God, the hypocrisy of the Christian slaveowner was not lost on the Negro. He notes in his spiritual that "everybody talkin' 'bout Heaven ain't goin' there."

You may take one spiritual and examine its content very carefully. For example, Run to Jesus can tell us much about the lives and thoughts of a slave. (Incidentally, Frederick Douglass claimed that Run to Jesus was his original inspiration for escaping from slavery. You may wish to raise the question: "Is this inconsistent with the remarks, from his Autobiography, on Christianity?") "Run to Jesus, shun the danger." Often slaves were forbidden to gather for worship and were thus forced to do so secretly in the woods at night. Slaves who were caught worshipping secretly might be severely punished. "I don't expect to stay much longer here . . . ." Slavery or life on earth was felt to be a temporary state. Jesus is on our side, and with His help we will gain our goal: freedom.

Spirituals reflect the hope and inspiration that religion provided. They also reflect that spirit which gave the Negro the strength to survive his overwhelming hardships. Social conditions are also reflected in spirituals. The hardships of slave labor and actual living environment may be revealed in a study of spirituals. Following is a list of spirituals which may be drawn from for a fuller look at Negro slave life as revealed by spirituals (recordings may be obtained for most of these).

Blow Your Trumpet Gabriel	Oh Mary Don't You Weep
Deep River	Oh When I Get To Heaven
The Gospel Train (Get on Board)	Sometimes I Feel Like a Motherless Child
Go Tell It on the Mountain	Steal Away
Goin' to Study War No More - (Down by the Riverside)	Swing Low Sweet Chariot
	Were You There
I'm A-Rolling (Through an Unfriendly World)	
I'm Just A-Goin Over Jordan	
Nobody Knows the Trouble I've Seen	

THE CHURCH AS REFUGE AND HOPE

The readings in this section are of two quite different types. Richard Allen's sermon reflects the emphasis of Negro Christianity before the Civil War. Students should be prepared to compare this sermon with the themes of the spirituals. E. Franklin Frazier's writing is part of a modern scholar's analysis of that earlier Negro Christianity of which Richard Allen was a part. Be sure to emphasize that Allen was no mere passive observer; rather, he was a vigorous, effective organizer for the proper institutional life of the black Christians in America. One must also note that other blacks saw the church not so much as "refuge" but as "obstacle" to the crushing of slavery and the winning of freedom. Note Walker's Appeal. A groundwork should be laid here so that the student is prepared for the harsh criticisms of Frederick Douglass later in the lesson. A good volume to consult in these connections is Benjamin Quarles, Black Abolitionists, Oxford University Press, 1969.

Richard Allen

1. The sermon of Richard Allen reflects both the attraction of Christianity for black slaves and the particular emphasis of black religion at this time.

   a. Be prepared to discuss why this emphasis would have special attraction in the 1830's and 1840's.

   b. Which spiritual does Allen's sermon most resemble? Be prepared to defend your choice.

Allen's sermon, as well as the spirituals, illustrates the special appeal of Christianity to the slave. Life on earth was but a prelude to life in heaven. As children of God, Christians were hopeful regarding a heavenly reward. As slaves, Negroes saw little evidence of rewards on earth. The Bible had a special appeal to an oppressed people whose circumstances were bleak. The black preachers of the ante-bellum period emphasized the point that black people were created in God's image. Thus the Christianity of the Negro reflected his unique needs and responded to his special longings.

Many spirituals parallel Allen's contention that with death "the power of the most cruel master ends, and all sorrow and tears are wiped away." Notable are the sentiments of spirituals 3, 5, 7. Students, by "paralleling" Allen and the spirituals, can reveal their understanding of the particular emphasis of Negro religion. Whichever spiritual a student chooses, he should be prepared to show how that one most resembles Allen's sermon.

E. Franklin Frazier

1. E. Franklin Frazier states that the "pent-up emotions and frustrations" of blacks found an outlet in the church.

    a. Why would black emotions be "pent-up"?

    b. How might the church provide such an outlet?

The Negro had to suffer the cruelty, confinement, and subjugation which slavery imposed. No protest was allowed. No release was provided. Though the aim of slaveowners might be the development of a nonthinking, docile, and obedient laborer, the human spirit could not be extinguished. While at work under the supervision of whites, the Negro could only harbor resentment or suffer silent rage. The slaveholding institution that broke up families, sold friends "down the river," and degraded the soul provoked feelings whose expression would bring sure punishment. Only when he was away from the white man could the black man express his inner feelings openly and honestly.

Negro religion provided one of the few opportunities for such expression. Unsupervised gatherings of any large number of slaves was, of course, forbidden. In the North freed Negroes could gather for worship. But whether open or secret, fellow sufferers could shout to heaven their innermost convictions. Black preachers, knowing full well what their flock had experienced during the week or in years past, were able to express common longings and common emotions. The singing of spirituals and the emotional responding to the preaching were high points of worship. The spontaneity and emotionalism of worship remained characteristic of the Negro church long after the abolition of slavery. For, as Frazier notes, the "pent up emotions and frustrations" also remained.

2. Frazier also talks of the Negro achieving "status" in the church.

    a. What is status?

    b. How might one find "status" in a church? Explain.

    c. Do you know men or women who today find "status" in their synagogues or churches? Have these people sought "status" for reasons similar to those of the nineteenth century slave? Why or why not?

A status is a position or rank to which one is assigned—in the minds of others—by virtue of birth or achievement. With the attainment of certain status, the individual acquires a prestige and a recognition satisfying to the ego. One might achieve status, that is, prestige or esteem, within the church even when status is not available outside of the church. The black man held low rank in the white-dominated society of the 1800's. He could not achieve a position where others would recognize his dignity or authority. Black effort and black ability were rewarded and recognized only in black society. And, for many decades black society was centered in the church.

Today many people find status in their synagogues or churches. Individuals may serve on governing boards; on finance, building, or other committees. They may teach Sunday School classes, conduct fund-raising campaigns, organize recreational activities, lead weekday prayer meetings or Bible-study groups, and engage in a variety of other activities in addition to participating in regular worship services. In each of these activities, an individual may assume a leadership role or a position of responsibility. In this manner, one may achieve "status." Prestige and self-esteem may follow.

The achievement of positions of responsibility, prestige or authority may bring with it great personal satisfaction. To know that one is doing much to serve God and fellowmen can be most rewarding. However, the particular reasons one seeks such status within religion or in any other realm are not easily known. For some, religion is the way to a genuine self-fulfillment. For others, religion as a kind of social service is particularly meaningful and satisfying. In some societies, of course, active identification with church and synagogue may be the way to lose "status" rather than gain it. In discussing this, students should explore the possible similarities between the nineteenth century Negro's involvement and that of modern Americans. They should also be made aware of the variety of needs which institutional religion may meet.

THE CHURCH DIVIDED AND REPROACHED

After students examine the three opposing statements on slavery (Methodist, Baptist, and Presbyterian), have them prepare for discussion. The discussion should (1) clarify the arguments based on religion for and against slavery and (2) explore the nonreligious factors which may have led to those arguments.

1. Arguments over slavery
   After reading the statements below about the white churches and slavery, assemble the arguments both for and against slavery.

   a. Which points have a religious basis?

   b. Which points are "nonreligious" in nature?

   Pro-slavery arguments:

   a. Abolitionists are motivated by economic and political considerations; also, abolitionists ascribe to a false philosophy or false (nonscriptural) principles.

   b. Negroes are unlearned and are given to lusts and passion. If given freedom, Negroes would injure themselves and others; thus, slavery is for their own good.

c. Slavery is no sin; it is not condemned in the Bible. God committed Negroes to "our charge" as servants.

Anti-slavery arguments:

a. Treating human beings as property is a violation of the law of God and is a sin.

b. Slavery is a violation of man's nature and of the Christian law of love.

c. Slavery is a moral, political, physical and social evil. It is the churches' duty to eliminate it.

2. Note the change in the Presbyterian position from 1818 to 1835. (Similar changes occurred in other churches.) What factors might account for this change?

At the beginning of the nineteenth century religious opposition to slavery was general, North and South. Before 1830, antislavery societies and propaganda prospered more in the South than in the North. All recognized that sudden emancipation would create many problems, but all agreed that gradual emancipation was a necessary aim. However, around 1830 Christians began to differ, at first quietly, later with rancor and bitterness.

Slavery was at this time suffering worldwide abandonment and attack. All European nations and all South American countries, except Brazil and Dutch Guiana, had forbidden slavery.

At the same time the Southern economy, boosted by the introduction of the cotton gin, had become dependent on slavery. Or so it seemed to many Southerners. Placed on the defensive, the South, joined by some in the North, began to rationalize and support the "dark and gloomy business." Concurrently, the North, joined by some in the South, accelerated the campaign against the "peculiar institution." After 1830 as the voice of the abolitionists became stronger and more strident, apologists and secessionists grew more extreme.

At first churchmen defended slavery as morally neutral. Later, slavery was defended as soundly Biblical. The existence of slavery in ancient Israel and even in New Testament times was frequently pointed out. Finally, slavery was defended on economic and moral grounds as a positive good, providing benevolence and discipline for the African race.

Gradually, positions, North and South, became more entrenched. Passions became more inflamed. For some church groups, division seemed inevitable.

The following account describes the step-by-step rationalizing defense of slavery. The passage is taken from the Autobiography (1856) of Peter Cartwright (1785-1872), probably the most famous Methodist frontier preacher. (You may wish to have students react to this statement.)

> Methodism increased and spread; and many Methodist preachers, taken from comparative poverty, not able to own a negro, and who preached loudly against it, improved and became popular among slaveholders; and many of them married into those slaveholding families. . . . Then they began to apologize for the evil; then to justify it, on legal principles; then on Bible principles; till lo and behold! it is not an evil but a good! it is not a curse but a blessing! till really you would think, to hear them, you would go to the devil for not enjoying the labor, toil, and sweat of this degraded race—and all this without rendering them any equivalent whatever!

3. Some churches, such as the Quakers, never did alter their original position. Why?

Some churches, it should be noted, did not change their original positions on slavery. The reasons for this were many and varied with each denomination. The Quakers (Friends) for one maintained a consistent stand on slavery. The following should be considered among the probable reasons for this:

    a. Quakers never were strong in the South except in North Carolina where there were fewer slaves. (But see the Journal of John Woolman.)

    b. Quakers maintained a particular sensitivity to social concerns and conscientiousness in moral behavior.

    c. The Quaker doctrine of "Inner Light" required the Friends to recognize something of God in all men—and therefore an intrinsic equality of all men.

Frederick Douglass

Frederick Douglass' Autobiography clearly reveals the religious attitude of a black American raised as a Christian and a slave. Several guiding questions are provided to help students understand Douglass' main theme and to relate this theme to present-day American religion.

1. What church is Douglass opposed to? Why?

Douglass is opposed to the Christian churches, North or South, who by their words and deeds support slavery. This is not the true Christianity of Christ, he argues. To be loyal to the Christianity of Christ demands hostility to the "Christianity of this land."

2. What does he mean by "partial" and "impartial" Christianity?

Christianity, Douglass points out, should be impartial. People of all colors or races should be welcomed into Christ's church on an equal basis. Partial Christianity is that corruption of Christ's church whereby people are treated differently according to social status or skin color.

3. Why does Douglass use words such as hypocritical, misnomer, fraud, libel? How does he support use of these words?

Douglass' central theme is that a slaveholding Christianity is a phony Christianity. Instead, many white Americans pretend to be Christians and proclaim their adherence to Christ's teachings. All the while they are engaging in practices completely contrary to Christianity. Thus, a Christianity that defends slavery is a sham. Douglass cites the cruel activities during the week of slaveholders who then on Sunday present themselves as worthy Christians.

4. Note that Douglass condemns that type of Christianity which is "in union with slaveholders." What evidence can you find that many Christians actively opposed slavery in this period?

The emphasis here should be upon the role that Christian churches (White and Black) and individual Christians played in abolitionism, in the underground railroad, in educating the Negro and so forth. See, for example, Timothy L. Smith, Revivalism and Social Reform (New York: Harper & Row), chapters 12, 13; and John Hope Franklin, From Slavery to Freedom (New York: Alfred A. Knopf, Inc., 1967), chapters 13-15, 21.

CHRISTIANITY ABANDONED AND CHRISTIANITY CHALLENGED

Malcolm X

Questions are provided to guide students to significant elements in the selection from Malcolm X.

1. What has Christianity done to the black man, according to Malcolm X?

Christianity "brainwashed" the black man into accepting a position of inferiority, into assuming the superiority of all things white. As a result, black people were deceived into accepting a role in society which denied to them their proper place.

2. What reasons can you infer for his leaving Christianity?

One may infer from this reading that Malcolm X left Christianity because it was a white man's religion. The whites used Christianity to insure the subservience of black men. Christianity could not provide the faith that the black man required. Black people needed a religion which would help them realize a better life in this world. Religion must help black men leave their inferior social position, not hinder them in their efforts to rise.

3. Is there anything in Malcolm X's writing that indicates it was written in the 1960's rather than the 1850's? If so, what?

This question is designed to have students consider the changes, if any, in the position of American Negroes vis-a-vis white Christians in 1850 and 1960. Except for a few minor allusions, Malcolm X's writing could well have been the work of a disenchanted black man a century ago.

Martin Luther King

Martin Luther King's 1963 speech from the steps of the Lincoln Memorial is not directed primarily to Negro religion. It does illustrate, however, as did the march on Washington itself, a new and vital role played by black churches and churchmen.

1. What challenge does Dr. King throw down to the churches?

Dr. King challenges the churches to bring America into line with its basic articles of faith. This challenge is hurled at all religious groups: black or white, Jew or Gentile, Protestant or Catholic. The task will be difficult, but with its completion will come new meaning to America's creed.

2. How does Dr. King (as compared with Richard Allen) see his role as a clergyman?

In his activity as a clergyman, Dr. King assumes a greater variety of responsibilities than Richard Allen would ever have attempted or thought possible. Allen's emphasis was pulpit preaching and preparing his flock to endure present hardships and reap the harvests in a life to come. Martin Luther King went out from the pulpit to lead his people in achieving on this earth a better life consistent with Christian principles. Dr. King concerned himself not only with the personal salvation of his flock but with the improvement of all society.

It should be noted that King's role would have been more difficult to assume in 1830. Conversely, some clergymen feel that their role today should be more like that of Allen. Dr. King's perception of a wider role for black clergymen is mirrored in the assumption of new roles by the Negro church. Whereas in Allen's day the church was primarily a refuge in a hostile white society, the modern church may be considered more a battle station or outpost from which black Americans may go forth to claim their birthright.

CONTEMPORARY PARALLEL

Students should be aware of major developments among black churchmen since the events referred to in this study. Perhaps the most influential single event was the dramatic appearance of James Forman at Riverside Church on April 26, 1969, when the Black Manifesto was first introduced. This Manifesto is an excellent modern-day parallel to the criticism of the churches expressed in the Frederick Douglass reading. A profitable research assignment would be a report on the response that the churches have made to the Manifesto. Reports on leaders such as James Forman, Eliezer Risco, and Muhammed Kenyatta would also be appropriate. Another recent development in the black churches is the introduction of "black theology." James H. Cone, the most important black theologian, writes, "In a society where men are oppressed because they are black, Christian theology must become Black Theology, a theology that is unreservedly identified with the goals of the oppressed community and seeking to interpret the divine character of their struggle for liberation."[1]

An important related question in this study is the role of the church in the lives of other important minority groups in this country—the 350,000 Indians and twelve million Spanish-Americans. What has been the influence of the church in the lives of these people? A report on the charismatic Cesar Chavez, leader of the Chicanos in the grape pickers' strike in Delano, California, would be an excellent "way in" to understanding the role of the church in the lives of Spanish-Americans. Although Chavez (like 90 percent of his fellow Spanish-Americans) is a Roman Catholic, he has great respect for the Protestant migrant ministry's work in the farmworkers' struggle. In a recent interview, he noted that the Protestant migrant ministry "was the first to come to our aid financially and in every other way." Recent evidence indicates that the Roman Catholic Church is beginning to push for economic and social justice for its Spanish-speaking flock. One of the most significant proofs of this involvement is the recent role of the National Conference of Catholic Bishops' in mediating the five-year-old labor strike between Chavez's group and the California growers.

A "case study" that should have particular appeal to students is the conflict between the Young Lords, a Puerto Rican counterpart of the Black Panthers, and the East Harlem First Spanish United Methodist Church. The Young Lords are besieging the First Church for use of its facilities for a program of free breakfasts for hungry children of the neighborhood. Students can locate reports of this conflict in the Reader's Guide.

Study and discussion of these questions should help students become aware of the influence of the church in the lives of minority groups in this country.

SUGGESTED ACTIVITIES

1. Choose and be able to defend one of the following statements.

   a. Christianity is (is not) meeting the needs of black Americans in the latter half of the twentieth century.

   b. The kind of activity which Martin Luther King called for is (is not) appropriate for the church, Negro or white.

---
[1] James H. Cone, A Black Theology of Liberation (Philadelphia: J. B. Lippincott Co., 1970), p. 11.

This activity calls for the development of a position statement by each student. Students will need to draw upon previous class discussions to fully develop their positions as the readings can only provide a starting point. Students should be encouraged to seek additional information to support their positions. Periodical articles, position statements of religious bodies and interviews which clergymen would constitute the most available resources. It should be stressed to students that they be able to explain why (citing supporting information) they chose their respective positions. See the bibliography and audio-visual resource suggestions at the end of this lesson.

Suggestions for Further Research

These areas of investigation are suggested for those students wishing to do additional research. In guiding students in their individual efforts, be sure to use the "Basic Library" as well as the Resource Guide below.

a. Determine whether Roman Catholicism is having a greater or lesser appeal to the Negro community today than a generation ago.

b. About one million American Negroes are members of smaller denominations or sects. Investigate the history and ritual of any two of these less familiar groups.

VOCABULARY

abstract	exploitation	irreconcilable	rebuke
affiliation	fetters	misnomer	reproach
alien	flagrant	perpetration	revivals
compensate	fraud	Pharisees	status quo
concrete	hypocritical	pollution	toto
countenance	imperative	precepts	unanimity
disinherited	indulgence	ravages	wholesale
dominion			

RESOURCE GUIDE FOR STUDY 6

I. Audio Visual Aids

A. Films

Brotherhood of Man. 10 min., color, rental $3.50
  Contemporary Films, 267 W. 25th St., New York, N.Y. 10001
An animated film designed to show that all types of people must live together in the world today. Narrator disproves the differences in races and shows that environment is all important.

Burden of Truth. 67 min., b&w, rental: free loan
  United Steel Workers of America, 1500 Commonwealth Bldg., Pittsburgh, Pa.
Tracing the life of a young Negro man, this film follows his work in the South, college life, marriage and employment in the North. Problems related to his acceptance, search for employment, search for housing and interpersonal relationships are described, and troubles experienced by him and the white person who befriends him are depicted.

Cast the First Stone. 42 min., b&w, rental: service charge
   Anti-Defamation League, 315 Lexington Ave., New York, N.Y. 10016
Narrated by John Daly, this documentary presents interviews with people of all walks of life as they confront racial prejudice. The bulk of the film deals with segregation of the Negro, but barriers thrown up before Puerto Rican, Polish, Jewish and Italian minority groups are also visualized.

Crisis in the Nation: White Racism. 90 min., b&w, rental $4.00
   Broadcasting and Film Commission (TV films), 475 Riverside Drive, Room 852, New York, N.Y. 10027
3 half-hour programs originally produced on NBC-TV. Part I: Discussion of housing and education problems. Part II: Discussion of jobs and economic development. Part III: Discussion of the Report of the National Advisory Commission.

Helen Tamiras in Negro Spirituals. 17 min., rental $12.50
   Contemporary Films, 267 W. 25th St., New York, N.Y. 10001
Modern dance interpretation of five spirituals.

History of the Negro in America, 1619–1860: Out of Slavery. 20 min., b&w, rental $4.80
   McGraw-Hill (Text-film Dept.), 330 W. 42nd St., New York, N.Y. 10009
The film traces the development of the African slave trade and the growth of slavery in the American colonies. It then presents the Negro's part in the American Revolution, slave labor as the foundation of Southern wealth, and the everyday life of the Negro, North and South. The Negro's resistance to slavery and his role in the abolitionist movement are traced. Film ends on the eve of the Civil War.

History of the Negro in America, 1861–1877: Civil War and Reconstruction. 20 min., b&w, rental $4.80
   McGraw-Hill (Text-film Dept.), 330 W. 42nd St., New York, N.Y. 10009
The political conflict over slavery, the root cause of the Civil War, opens this film. It depicts what the Negro did to help win his own freedom. Discussed are the Emancipation Proclamation, the passage of the 13th, 14th, and 15th Amendments, and the story of Reconstruction.

History of the Negro in America, 1877–Today: Freedom Movement. 20 min., b&w, rental $4.80
   McGraw-Hill (Text-film Dept.), 330 W. 42nd St., New York, N.Y. 10009
The Negro, abandoned by the North and shut out of political life in the South, is forced into a share-cropper-tenant farmer life. Some migrate to the North and the West. But everywhere, there are segregation laws. He fights in World War I and World War II but is denied democracy at home. A great cultural renaissance for the "new Negro" takes place in the 1920's. Since 1950, his stepped-up battle for civil rights has stirred the conscience of the nation.

Nothing But a Man. 92 min. Rental (sliding scale)
   Audio Film Center, 34 MacQuesten Parkway, Mount Vernon, N.Y., 10550
A very fine account of a Black man's struggle to be accepted as a human being in a hostile environment.

Requiem. color, rental $10.00
   Mass Media Ministries, 2116 North Charles St., Baltimore, Maryland 21218
"Free at last. Free at last. Thank God Almighty, I am free at last." These are the words on the gravestone of Martin Luther King, Jr., to whom this film is dedicated. It shows the constant and bitter struggle of his life. The struggle which was not merely a personal one, but was symbolic of millions of people around the world.

Walk in My Shoes. 54 min., b&w, rental $10.90
McGraw-Hill (Text-film Dept.), 330 W. 42nd St., New York, N.Y. 10009
The film explores the world of the Negro and listens to him as he speaks in many voices. He speaks for and against the Black Muslims, Martin Luther King, Freedom Riders, integration, and the NAACP.

We Hold These Truths. 28 min., b&w, rental $8.00
NCC Broadcasting and Film Commission, 475 Riverside Dr., New York, N.Y. 10027
The question of American's "inalienable rights" confuses a Negro soldier, about to sail for combat, as to what he is fighting for. A chaplain friend, seeing the young man's dilemma, suggests he visit the East Harlem Protestant Parish in New York City. There he discovers a measure of clarity as he sees the church at work seeking to meet the problem of his people.

B. Filmstrips

Balm in Gilead. 113-frame filmstrip, color, sale: $5.00
West Side Christian Parish, 1544 W. Roosevelt Road, Chicago 8, Illinois
This documentary filmstrip describes a Chicago inner city district with many immigrant and southern Negro residents, then relates the work of the West Side Christian Parish which attempts to meet the social, economic, and spiritual needs through a group ministry.

The House of Decision. 180-frame filmstrip, color, rental $1.00, sale $20.00
United Church of Christ Bureau of Audio-Visuals, 1501 Race St., Philadelphia, Pa. 19102
An educated, middle-class Negro family search for better housing in an unsegregated neighborhood. They face all the prejudices and insults usually thrown their way as white persons look at their color but not at them as persons.

C. Recordings

The Autobiography of Frederick Douglass, Folkways No. 5522 ($5.79) Narrated by Ossie Davis.

Fisk Jubilee Singers, Folkways No. 2372 ($5.79)
Early spirituals are sung by the famous Fish University "Jubilee Singers." Organized in 1871, this group of black students introduced the spiritual to many Americans and, later, Europeans.

The Glory of Negro History, Folkways No. 7752 ($5.79)
Written and recorded by Langston Hughes. Documentary from Columbus through the UN.

Songs of the American Negro Slaves, Folkways No. 5252 ($5.79)
Sung by Michel LaRue. The album includes documentary notes by Negro scholar John Hope Franklin.

We Shall Overcome, Folkways No. 5591 ($5.79)
Spirituals, gospels, and new songs about civil rights are sung by various black groups.

The above records may be ordered from Folkways/Scholastic Records, 906 Sylvan Avenue, Englewood Cliffs, New Jersey, 07632.

Marian Anderson Sings Spirituals, RCA Victor LM-2032 ($5.79)

Tuskegee Institute Choir—Spirituals, Westminster 14989 ($4.98)
  Spirituals are sung by another famous Negro group.

Deep River and Other Spirituals, RCA Victor LM/LSC-2247 ($5.79)
  Arrangements sung by the Robert Shaw Chorale.

Negro Spirituals, Capitol (S) P-8600 ($5.79)
  Arrangements sung by the Roger Wagner Chorale.

The above recordings may be ordered through most record dealers.

March on Washington: The Official Album. Produced by station WRVR, Riverside Church, New York City.
The Speech of Martin Luther King and several others recorded; dramatic and effective.

II. Articles

"Big Day: End and a Beginning," Newsweek, vol. 62 (September 9, 1963).
  The March on Washington with the "I Have a Dream" speech by Martin Luther King.

"Black Power: Gospel of Black Nationalism," Newsweek, vol. 71 (January 15, 1968).

"Black Revolt in White Churches," Ebony, vol. 23 (September, 1968).

"Case of Conscience," Sports Illustrated, vol. 24 (May 9, 1966).
  Cassius Clay (Mohammud Ali) and his involvement with the Black Muslims and his fighting career. An interesting slant on the Black Muslim movement.

"Church and the Negro," America, vol. 117 (July 8, 1967).

"Church and the Urban Negro," America, vol. 118 (February 10, 1968).

"I'm Talking to You, White Man; Excerpt from Autobiography of Malcolm X," Saturday Evening Post, vol. 237 (September 12, 1964).

"Lord of the Doves," Newsweek, vol. 69 (April 17, 1967).
  Martin Luther King's protest against the war in Vietnam.

"Mississippi: After Violence a Ray of Hope," Ebony, vol. 20 (June, 1965).

"My Husband Died for Democracy: Minister Killed in Cleveland Rights Protest," Ebony, vol. 19 (June, 1964).

"Mystery of Malcolm X," Ebony, vol. 19 (September, 1964).

"Negro Worship and Universal Need," Christian Century, vol. 83 (March 30, 1966).
  The possibility of the White Church borrowing from the Black.

"New Negro Threat: Mass Disobedience," U.S. News and World Report, vol. 63 (August 28, 1967).

"The Quest for the Black Christ," Ebony, vol. 24 (March, 1969).
An excellent article on the Black Church searching for its identity and its relationship to Black nationalism, etc.

"Search for a Black Past," Life, vol. 65 (November 22, 1968; November 29, 1968; December 6, 1968; and December 13, 1968).

"They Come Marching Up Conscience Road; Negroes Stir Up Nation in Mighty Washington March," Life, vol. 55 (September 6, 1963).

"Third Force in Christendom; Gospel Singing, Dooms-day Preaching Sects," Life, vol. 44 (June 9, 1958).

"Why I Quit the Convent," Ebony, vol. 24 (December, 1968).
A Black woman's account of her involvement with White church institutions.

III. Books

Bennett, Lerone. What Manner of Man; A Biography of Martin Luther King, Jr., 1929-1968. Chicago: Johnson. $5.95

Breitman, George. The Last Year of Malcolm X: The Evolution of a Revolutionary. New York: Schocken Books. (paper) $1.95

Cohen, Henry. Justice, Justice: A Jewish View of the Black Revolution. New York: Union of American Hebrew Congregations. (paper) $2.75

Cone, James H. Black Theology and Black Power. New York: Seabury Press. (paper) $2.95

Douglass, Frederick. Narrative of the Life of Frederick Douglass An American Slave, Written by Himself. New York: New American Library. (paper) $0.50

Fisher, Miles M. Negro Slave Songs in the United States. New York: Russell and Russell Publishers. $9.50

Franklin, John Hope. From Slavery to Freedom: A History of Negro Americans. Third Edition. New York: Alfred A. Knopf, 1967.

Gordis, Robert. Race and the Religious Tradition. New York: Anti-Defamation League of B'nai B'rith. (28 p.) $0.25

Johnson, James and J. Rosamond Johnson. Books of American Negro Spirituals. New York: Viking Press. $6.95

Katz, William L. Teachers' Guide to American Negro History. Chicago: Quadrangle Books. $2.45
Designed specifically for the social studies curriculum in the secondary schools. This volume is simply indispensable for teachers handling topics dealing with the black experience in America.

Malcolm X. and Alex Haley. The Autobiography of Malcolm X. New York: Grove Press. (paper) $1.25

Mathews, Donald G. Slavery and Methodism. Princeton: Princeton University Press, $7.50

Miller, William R. Martin Luther King, Jr.: His Life, Martyrdom, and Meaning for the World. New York: Weybright and Talley. $7.95

Vorspan, Albert. Giants of Justice. New York: Union of American Hebrew Congregations. $3.75

──── and Eugene J. Lipman. Justice and Judaism: The Work of Social Action. Rev. ed. New York: Union of American Hebrew Congregations. $3.50

Washington, Joseph R., Jr. Black Religion: The Negro and Christianity in the United States. Boston: Beacon Press. (paper) $2.45

Woolman, John. Journal of John Woolman, Plea for the Poor. New York: Citadel Press (paper) $1.75 Reveals Woolman's personal Quaker protest against slavery.

(In the Basic Library, particular attention is called to the following volumes:

Frazier, The Negro Church in America

Mead, Handbook of Denominations)

7
RELIGION: PERSONAL AND SOCIAL

THE PLAN OF THE STUDY

Introduction—Psychology and Sociology of Religion

Personal Religion

Hasidism: Religion Personal and Social

Social Religion

Organized Religion and American Society

Middletown: A Case for a Panel Discussion

Contemporary Parallel

Suggested Activities

Vocabulary

Resource Guide

THE FOCUS OF THIS STUDY

In this study students investigate two dimensions of religion in America: the psychological and the sociological. They will find that religion is personal. It influences an individual's attitudes and values, his daily behavior, his outlook on life. A study of the effect of religion on an individual is a study of the psychology of religion. Additionally, students will find that religion is social. It influences the structure and functioning of society. As students explore the effects of religion upon social institutions, they learn something of the sociology of religion.

THE OBJECTIVES FOR THIS STUDY

Knowledge Objectives—Each student will demonstrate his knowledge that:

1. Religion directly influences individual thoughts and behavior (psychological dimension) and the social order (sociological dimension).

2. Social religion and personal religion, while often distinguishable, are neither separate nor antithetical but, rather, they are complimentary.

3. American religious leaders responded vigorously to the problems of industrial America, and continue to do so.

4. New religious organizations and progressive programs were born in response to perceptions of social problems.

5. While some religious leaders hold that either personal conversion or social reform is inadequate as the sole approach to human improvement, others emphasize the adequacy of conversion or regeneration.

6. Many Americans see a Judaeo-Christian ethic as superior to the ethics of self-interest or of the marketplace and this belief has direct implications for their behavior and for the concerns of social organizations in which they participate.

7. Disagreements within religious traditions over emphases upon personal conversion and social reform continue today as serious, controversial issues.

Skill Objectives—Each student will demonstrate his ability to:

1. Analyze writings for elements of agreement and disagreement.

2. Distinguish ends from means in programs for human betterment.

3. Carefully study the commitments and concerns of individuals and groups in order to make inferences about how they might react in new situations or about what positions they might take upon new issues.

4. Identify the activities of a religious group as attempts to influence directly a) individual behavior or b) the social order.

5. Cope with judgments on open-ended, value-ladened questions, taking a stand and offering a justification in dialogue with classmates.

6. Identify different alternative lifestyles and commitments as to their implications in differing judgments and actions on great social issues and everyday matters.

Value and Attitude Objectives—Each student will demonstrate his willingness to:

1. Inquire with an open-mind toward religious commitments and arguments that are unfamiliar or different from one's own.

2. Inquire with empathy for religious leaders and organizations as they wrestle with the issues noted in this Study—an empathy based upon an understanding of the commitments of these leaders and organizations.

3. Reflect upon one's own feelings (emotions) toward the issues noted in this Study and attempt to explain one's feelings and their appropriateness.

4. Reflect upon one's own commitments vis-a-vis several alternatives, as to their implications for decision-making on ethical questions and for conceptions of a "better society."

INTRODUCTION

The introductory section of this Study employs a brief expository passage to state the issue for students. In class discussion, students should define "personal religion" and "social religion" and give examples from their own experience. This exploratory discussion provides an opportunity for students to see the direct relevance of the historical material, which follows in the Study, to their own time. Later, after working through the student material and the Middletown activity, the teacher might draw upon suggestions in the "contemporary parallel" section of this Guide to involve students in the current manifestations of the issue.

PERSONAL RELIGION

Though no Catholic or Jewish writings are used in this part of the study, students should understand that personal religion is far from an exclusively Protestant approach. Thomas Merton, a Trappist monk, presents an outstanding Catholic viewpoint in The Seven-Story Mountain. A Jewish view of personal religion is set forth in Martin Buber's The Origin and Meaning of Hasidism.

Revivalism

The revivalists present one type of personal religion. To the present they have played a conspicuous role in America's history. Their brand of personal religion emphasized biblical authority and personal conversion. The readings contained in this lesson were chosen to give students a "feel" for a major religious tradition in American history.

The following study questions will direct student reading and serve as the basis for class discussion. Students should consider the nature of "conversion" as espoused by the revivalists.

1. What did the conversion experience do for Finney? What do you, from this account, consider to be the nature of the conversion experience?

There are, of course, many explanations from psychological to theological for Finney's experience. Finney had evidently suffered much inner turmoil, torment and anxiety. The sources of this suffering were the basic questions of existence. Who am I? How should I live? What should I live for? What of life after death? In his conversion experience Finney resolved these questions to his own satisfaction. After conversion, Finney was convinced he was "on the right track."

You might ask students if this gives them some clues as to the nature of such an experience. (Note that the word "convert" means to turn, to change, to shift directions.)

2. Would you consider Moody's understanding of the nature of conversion to be the same as Finney's? Why or why not?

Finney and Moody are in agreement that conversion or regeneration is the very foundation of their religious lives. Finney found it necessary to be "reborn" for his own salvation. Moody, quoting the Bible, states that without regeneration a man "cannot see the kingdom of God." Both see this personal transformation as something which God works in the life of man. One's life is, thereafter, sharply divided—as sharply divided as existence in the womb is from life after natural birth.

3. In what ways are the themes of Moody and Graham similar?

Both Moody and Graham believe conversion to be absolutely necessary for the salvation of man. Both see in conversion the way to a better world (Moody, the "kingdom of God"; Graham, the "Kingdom Society"). Unless there is "rebirth," no better world will come about. The third chapter of the Gospel according to St. John also has similar meaning for the two revivalists.

4. Judging from the selection by Billy Graham, what characteristics of modern man (and society) need changing?

Self-interest, hate, taking advantage, conniving, swindling—all these must be eliminated. "National greed and selfishness are the corporate expressions of self-interest. . . ."

5. Why—again according to Graham—can't a "great society" be realized without conversion?

There must be an inner change in men. Without this change no "great society" will ever arrive. Graham says that self-interest can produce no superior social order. Greed and selfishness must go. "Fallible men cannot create an infallible society. . . ." With conversion, the shortcomings of men disappear; then "new men" can begin building the "great society."

New Institutions

The material on The Salvation Army presents another personal approach to religion. Additional viewpoints are indicated in the bibliography. The questions about The Salvation Army direct students to significant considerations. No discussion of these questions is planned; however, you may wish to help students clarify the special nature of The Salvation Army.

1. What type of "ministering" does The Salvation Army engage in?

In addition to the teaching and preaching activities common to most religious groups, the Army concentrates on reaching the physically down-trodden and spiritually disheartened members of society. Victims of social ills and personal misfortune are the special beneficiaries of the Army's ministry. The Army has ministered to the poverty-stricken, the jobless, the transient, the alcoholic, the addicted, the imprisoned, the hospitalized, the abandoned, the demoralized—in short, the needy.

2. Does this make it different from other churches? If so, how?

The Army's concentration upon basic human needs has demanded a special organization. The Army was drawn up along military lines by its founder, William Booth. This was necessary, Booth felt, because the Army "invaded" territories where few other "good people" would tread. The roughest of neighborhoods, the most wicked of dens, the most horrible slums—these places had proved too challenging, too forbidding to others. But Booth's "soldiers" with dogged determination set up "outposts"—soup kitchens, infirmaries, sleeping quarters, rehabilitation centers—right where they were needed most.

3. What justification is there for saying The Salvation Army is representative of "personal" rather than "social" religion?

The Army seeks to reach the individual, and conversion is an important goal of the Army's work. Personal needs are paramount. Operating on a face-to-face basis, the Army has little to say about changing the basic social, political, and economic order. Though the Army would have all live by Judaeo-Christian principles, it would seek to realize this through a personal ministry.

HASIDISM: RELIGION PERSONAL AND SOCIAL

In this section students have the opportunity to examine a tradition which combines the personal and the social, without emphasis on either and stresses the unity of life—the wholeness of reality.

1. What element is common to all movements that may be called "Hasidic"?

The common element is the desire to take seriously their piety—"their relation to the divine in earthy life" and their lives together on earth based upon divine teachings.

2. What do you think Buber means by "soul-force"?

The term, "the soul-force of Judaism," means the divine manifest in life on earth: the "inner truth" that "God can be beheld in each thing and <u>reached</u> through each pure deed"; the divine spark that can be uncovered by pure action.

3. From Buber's brief summary, what aspects of Hasidism seem mainly personal? What aspects mainly social?

The social form is Hasidism as a "great popular community" acting, not in withdrawal or isolation, but in the world together. But students should see that Hasidism stresses the unity, the wholeness, of faith and work. The distinction between "social" and "personal" is not applicable.

4. How useful or important is it in Hasidism to distinguish between the personal and the social?

Given Hasidism's unity and the stress upon the divine, it is not useful or important to make the distinction between "personal" and "social." The personal and social are one—life as faith as one—"One must serve God with one's whole life, with the whole of the everyday, with the whole of reality." Students might reflect here on the current discussions of person's responding to others as "whole persons." Also, the current use of "soul" in the black community makes an interesting comparison with Buber's "soul-force."

Two additional sources are useful for teachers and students who want to read more about Hasidism:

Martin Buber. <u>The Origin and Meaning of Hasidism</u>. New York: Harper & Row, Publishers, 1960. Paperback.

Jerome R. Mintz. <u>Legends of the Hasidim</u>. Chicago: University of Chicago Press, 1968. Illustrated.

SOCIAL RELIGION

Social religion, like personal religion, finds strong support among Catholics and Jews, as well as Protestants. As noted in the student materials, social religion has deep roots in the Judaeo-Christian heritage.

Students may seek some interpretation of the passage of Amos. Amos denounces the pious merchant-farmers who are concerned only with gain. They observe the ritual, but not the substance of religion. They do not do business on holy days, but they cannot wait until these days have passed so they might once again make money. In their business they may deceive the customer, "making the ephah small" (the ephah was an ancient Hebrew unit of dry measure approximately equal to a bushel). At the same time they charge all that the traffic will bear, "making the shekel great" (the shekel was a Hebrew unit of money).

The readings in this lesson reflect a similar concern to that of the prophet Amos for social justice. The readings are of the decades 1900-1920, a time when social religion in America was in large part a response to the industrialization and urbanization of the country. The authors particularly emphasize, therefore, reform in socio-economic theory and practices. Students should know, however, that social religion concerns itself with the reform of the whole society, not merely the economic structures.

The Social Gospel

1. How is Gladden's attitude similar to that of the prophet Amos?

Amos condemned those men who professed religion, followed the little laws, but failed to display the true spirit of the Hebrew faith. Gladden, too, was disturbed by "good Christians," who lack the true Christian spirit, holding to philosophies which fatten their pocketbooks, but belie their Christianity.

2. What is Gladden's feeling toward "regeneration"? How does this compare with Moody's attitude?

For Gladden, regeneration is not enough. Converted Christians may, unfortunately, hold to false philosophies which, whatever they contribute to material prosperity, do nothing to "Christianize" the social order.

Moody, however, felt that regeneration changed men's heads as well as hearts.

3. What must the churches do in addition to changing men's hearts? Why, in your opinion, does Gladden take this position?

Gladden felt that men's minds must be changed as well as their hearts. Men must learn what is appropriate to the spirit of Christianity in the social order. Gladden lived in an age of gross exploitation of men by fellow men, of child labor, sweatshops, union busting, and the like. Economic practices then current seemed to deny a place for religious teaching in industrial relations.

Social Justice

1. What does Wise mean by a "minister going into politics"? What is his attitude toward this?

As he uses the phrase "a minister going into politics," Wise does not mean running for public office or holding a party position. Wise is talking about a minister taking a stand on civil issues. Since political action brings about reform, Wise advocates the use of clerical influences—through speaking, writing, organizational membership and leadership—on the formulation of public policies.

2. Wise quotes from the Hebrew Bible: "Justice, Justice shalt thou pursue." What do you think this means to Wise?

"Justice, Justice shalt thou pursue" is, obviously, a fundamental moral obligation for Wise. With all the resources at his disposal, Wise must work for social justice. This was for Wise the primary task of a "minister." There are no qualifications to the command; justice above all else must be pursued.

3. Concerning social justice and social equity, what must the churches and synagogues generally do? (Specifically, what might they do?)

The churches and snyagogues must respond to the problems of society. They "must demand and demand unceasingly an ever-increasing measure of social equity and social justice." Specifically, the churches and synagogues might formulate positions on social issues and then "speak out" as a moral force on those issues. Churchmen, clerical and lay, might participate in community efforts to bring about change. Churches might help in organizing social action groups to bring about better housing, better schools and better working conditions. Christian and Jewish leaders might work for recreation facilities, voting rights, prison reform and equal opportunity in a number of areas in which discrimination is common. They can mount campaigns to initiate and promote legislation, change public policies and procedures, and insure implementation of reform laws. Programs to awaken citizens and educate politicians might also be an ongoing concern of the churches and synagogues.

4. Why might the churches and synagogues be "farces of respectability and convention" rather than "forces of righteousness"? Is Rabbi Wise, in your opinion, being fair to the churches and synagogues? Why or why not?

The purpose behind this question is to have students think about the influence of society upon the churches and synagogues and about the gap between religious ideals and actual practices. Some considerations in answering the question may include the following:

  a. Some churches that were conservative and tradition-oriented had made little adjustment from an agrarian society to an industrial society that embodied a host of new social-economic relationships.

  b. Other churches or synagogues were more concerned about their social standing in a community than they were about correcting or improving society itself.

  c. To be more concerned about respectability than righteousness was to become a farce—just like Amos' merchants.

Social Action

1. What philosophy had developed in America that Ryan agrees (with the Bishops) is false?

The philosophy that supports unlimited property rights is false. This belief in absolute ownership of property is contrary to Catholic moral philosophy. Ryan emphasizes that man holds property as a trustee under God and is bound to use property (wealth, goods) for the good of all human beings. Man does not have the absolute right to exclude others from a portion of the earth's goods. He is only a steward of that which God has given.

2. What particular social issue has therefore drawn the attention of these clergymen?

Violent clashes between labor and capital had drawn the attention of the bishops. Labor was then challenging the capitalists' claims of sovereignty in determining the use and distribution of the "goods of the earth." Specifically, labor was demanding a greater share of the rewards.

3. What seems to be the objections to the Bishop's Program? Who is doing the objecting?

Some people have challenged the authority of the bishops to speak upon social and economic issues. These people feel no obligation—be they "good Catholics" or not—to follow the bishops. The objectors seem to support the position of industry and are in opposition to the bishops' call for more equity.

ORGANIZED RELIGION AND AMERICAN SOCIETY

1. What similarities exist in the three programs? What differences? Does "social religion" have distinctive denominational emphases or not? (Support your answer.)

The programs of Protestants and Jews are very similar. Both programs are offered to relieve the plight of industrial workers in the first two decades of the twentieth century. The programs commonly embody support for workmen's compensation, a shortened workday, one rest day per week, old age support, minimum wages, and arbitration procedures. They call for the abolition of child labor. The two statements show concern about the safety of workers and the status of women. Both call for a more equitable division of profits and products. Additionally, the Federal Council of Churches calls for the abatement of poverty and the suppression of sweatshops, while the Rabbis ask for public employment bureaus, housing for workers, and constructive care for dependents, mental defectives and criminals. They are also concerned about preserving home life.

The Bishops' Program of Social Reconstruction is not presented in full in the student materials. However, the concerns of the Bishops closely parallel those of Protestants and Jews. What is presented in the student materials is the concluding statement in their Program. In this statement they point out that in addition to reconstruction of social institutions and the reformation of economic relationships as advocated by all three groups, reform of the minds and hearts of men must also take place.

The strikingly similar concerns of Protestants and Jews (paralleled in the full text of the Bishops' Program) reveals that social religion is not a denominational phenomenon. Particular "causes" of Jews, such as child labor abolition, were also particular "causes" of Protestants and Catholics. While we could expect the Rabbis would be especially concerned with the plight of Jewish working girls who filled the sweatshops of the garment industry, Catholics and Protestants were no less adamant in their demands that women be especially protected from exploitation.

2. How much of the programs presented here has become reality?

Most points enumerated in the programs have now become law. Over the past five decades laws have been passed, programs have been developed, and groups have been organized to help realize the goals of the social action programs. (A few students might conduct individual research into the legislation since 1920 dealing with such matters as child labor, minimum wage, worker safety, length of workweek, collective bargaining, etc.)

3. Which of the goals have yet to be obtained?

Workers are yet to be protected from the hardships of economic crises, though proposals for a guaranteed annual wage gain increasing attention. Poverty is still with us and housing is still woefully inadequate. Perhaps the nonmaterial goals stated by the bishops are farthest from realization.

4. What might account for the realization of some but not of other goals?

There has been less agreement upon the validity of some goals. Also, certain goals, such as the "abatement of poverty" are more difficult to reach than, for example, the "enactment of an eight-hour day." Goals have been reached not only through growth of unions and government action, but also through technological change and continued prosperity.

5. Are there any goals that you feel are not appropriate or desirable? If so, which ones and why? Are there goals here which you think are not the business of organized religion? If so, which ones, and why?

Students may question the validity of some of the goals. Additionally, they may question whether some have truly been reached. For example, it is difficult to ascertain whether the "most equitable division of products" has been obtained. Individuals may disagree over what is "most equitable." Stress should be placed upon students explaining their own positions regarding desirable goals and the churches' involvement in reaching them.

MIDDLETOWN: A CASE FOR A PANEL DISCUSSION

Students who participate on the panel should be given plenty of time to prepare their discussion. Each should determine how he or she, as a representative of a particular religious tradition, may best contribute to the discussion. Each should do additional reading to deepen his understanding of the religious tradition he represents. (Have students consult the bibliography provided for you below.) The role of the moderator is very important. This person must be knowledgeable and should be neutral. But his neutrality is only in handling the discussion. The moderator, too, has a vital concern to find solutions to the town's problems. The moderator could be either a student or a teacher.

Some of the areas the panel could explore are:

1. Aid to individuals and families
2. Rehabilitation programs
3. Working with governmental and political party organizations
4. Working with industry and labor unions
5. Educational programs and youth groups
6. Revivals or "missionary" programs

Clergymen in the audience (the rest of the class) should be prepared to question, support, or challenge proposals made by the panel members. Later the class should evaluate the panel in terms of how well each panel member accurately portrayed his role. Conclusions should also be reached about the appropriate role (or roles) of religion in society.

CONTEMPORARY PARALLEL

This Study offers many opportunities for involving students in an understanding of the personal and social aspects of religion. Since all major religious groups are deeply involved in the controversies of personal and social aspects of religion, students could do "community" research of the conflict within their own religious traditions. Interviews with both laymen and clergy, young and old, reading the publications of their denomination, analyzing sermons and Sunday School lessons would be helpful. A report on the budget cut-backs of churches as a consequence of their involvement in social action would be revealing. For example, it has been estimated that the United Presbyterian Church may lose "a minimum of five million dollars" as a result of its $10,000 grant to Angela Davis' legal defense fund. What are the implications of these cut-backs? Perhaps students could research this financial aspect in their local churches. A number of groups have been organized both to focus the involvement of churches on social issues and to protest such involvement. Students could report on such groups as Clergy and Laymen Concerned About Vietnam, the National Center for Black Catholicism, or Concerned Presbyterians. An interesting assignment would be to compare the editoral stance of The Christian Century (liberal) and Christianity Today (conservative). Students could respond (perhaps as a panel) to the following observation on the role of the clergyman by David Lawrence, editor of U.S. News and World Report (as quoted in the June 3, 1965, issue of Christian Advocate):

> If the sermons were confined solely to spiritual matters, the layman would accept the interpretation given him as an expression of conscience. But when an argument is made that is related to a question of governmental policy, the layman, as emotions rise, begins to lose his awareness of a spiritual influence. . . . Many clergymen seem to have lost the halo of God's light and to have plunged into the darkness of life itself. What a tragic loss to the community in which this happens!

Dr. Jeffrey K. Hadden, sociologist, has undertaken the most thorough survey of Protestant beliefs, opinions, and attitudes ever compiled in his recent book, The Gathering Storm in the Churches (Garden City, New York: Doubleday & Company, Inc., 1969). Of particular interest to this study is his evidence documenting the alienation of clergy and laity on the issue of religion as "comfort" or "challenge." Hadden sees parallel developments within Roman Catholicism. What about similar conflicts in Judaism? Is there a parallel situation in those Jews who see Judaism primarily as a religion and those who stress Judaism as a nationality? Jewish theologian Leo Trepp observes that although "there is no great religious fervor" among American Jews, "yet there exists a feeling that one must work for Judaism. . . . The urge to do something has led to a proliferation of charitable, social, and service organizations that are sharply competitive with each other for membership and recognition."

A recent phenomenon that should be of considerable interest to students is the "Jesus Movement" or the "Jesus Freaks." Perhaps some students in the class are involved in this movement themselves. Does this movement identify more with the personal or social emphasis of religion?

Folk and rock music offers a wealth of commentary on this issue and should provide a superb source for intriguing assignments.

SUGGESTED ACTIVITIES

These areas of investigation are suggested for those students wishing to do additional research. In guiding students in their individual efforts, be sure to use the Basic Library as well as the Resource Guide below.

1. What are the various private ways that religious faith may express itself? How do these vary—or do they—from one religious tradition to another?

2. Investigate in detail one social action project of organized religion in your community. Who sponsors it? What form of activity is it? How effective is it? What resistance is there to it?

3. What religious phenomena are of particular interest to psychologists of religion?

4. Sociologists of religion pay special attention to what areas or aspects of religion?

VOCABULARY

accorded	contradictory	fulfillment	profit motive
alleviation	conversion	humanitarian	providence
arbitration	corporate	infallible	radical
bastion	deprivation	inviolable	redemption
benevolent	divisiveness	mediation	regeneration
capitalist	encroachments	pagan	righteousness
commercial	equitable	Pandemonium	squalor
conciliation	ethic	partisanship	stewardship
connive	fanaticism	pillage	tenets
consequence			

RESOURCE GUIDE FOR STUDY 7

I. Audio Visual Aids

A. Films

Almost Neighbors. 34 min., b&w, rental $10.00
   National Council of Churches, Broadcasting and Film Commission, 475 Riverside Drive, New York, N.Y. 10027
This film presents the Christian concept of "neighbor." Details of one white middle class family's reaction to the prospect of new neighbors. Also, what is the responsibility of the church? This film could be used an an introduction to the study. It serves well for motivation.

Blood and Fire. 30 min., b&w, rental $7.00
   National Film Board of Canada, 680 Fifth Avenue, New York, N.Y. 10019 or Contemporary Films, 267 W. 25th Street, New York, N.Y. 10001
The camera goes behind the scenes to show the Salvation Army at work. The evangelistic and welfare activities are presented in a "candid camera" approach. This film could well be used after the reading but prior to a discussion of the Army.

Conversion Plus. 40 min., b&w, rental $7.00 (color–$11.00)
   The Methodist Church, Cokesbury Bookstores, 201 Eighth Avenue S., Nashville, Tennessee 37203 (or regional offices)
By following the changes in the lives of a young, successful, middle class couple, the role of conversion in a Christian context is revealed. Teachers should exercise care in using this film. It presents one approach to religion, one approach to Christianity. Its contribution to a study of "Personal or Social Religion" lies in explaining, not advocating, conversion. If used, the film should be shown after students read the selection by Finney, Moody and Graham. Discussion of the readings and the film can then be combined. Stress should be placed on what conversion means to some Christians. For an extended disucssion, this film could be used in conjunction with The Work of My Hands (see below). This would, of course, demand careful previewing and discussion preparation.

The Newcomers. 25 min., b&w, rental $8.00
   The Methodist Church, Cokesbury Bookstores, 201 Eighth Avenue S., Nashville, Tennessee 37203 (or regional offices)
The focal point here is the adjustment problem of migrants to the city. The work of the churches in helping these people is revealed. The film could be used to illustrate an activity that contains social and personal elements. It could work well with a discussion of the contemporary foci of social religion.

Nineteen Trees. 14 min., rental: Service charge
   Anti-Defamation League, 315 Lexington Ave., New York, N.Y. 10016
Residents of a crowded degenerating neighborhood find a common concern in beautifying their block. In the course of planting trees they gain understanding of each other. This film would be an excellent culminating activity.

The Pugnacious Sailing Master. Eternal Light (kinescope). $8.50
   The story of Uriah P. Levy, who conducted a successful fight to abolish corporal punishment in the United States Navy.

Religious Revolution and the Void. 58 min., b&w, rental $10.00
   National Educational Television Film Service, Audio Visual Center, Indiana University, Bloomington, Indiana
This is a thorough examination of religion in American life. Traditional and experimental forms of religious activity are presented. Churchmen are shown dealing with problems of alienation, civil rights, the disadvantaged, etc. The full variety of religious approaches, including personal and social, are treated. This film is especially recommended to culminate this study. We suggest that it be used after completing the activities. Discussion could then follow.

The Sandpile: Social Action. 28 min., b&w, rental-apply
   Produced by CBS-TV. Available from Carousel Films, 1501 Broadway, New York, N.Y. 10036
Race relations and the role of the church in resolving racial issues are explored. The film could parallel discussion of the church's relevancy in present day.

This is God's World. 20 min., b&w, rental $4.00
   Protestant Episcopal Church, 815 Second Avenue, New York, N.Y. 10017
Again the relevancy of the church to modern society is explored. The experiences and reactions of six inner-city workers are pictured. Problems presented include unemployment, race and housing. This film, too, brings social action up-to-date. Thus it could well follow the readings on social religion.

Tomorrow? 27 min., b&w, rental $8.00
   United Church of Christ, 1501 Race Street, Philadelphia, Pa. 19102
This film explores the future in terms of technological change and resultant social and economic upheaval. What is the role of the church in the new industrial revolution? As a culminating activity, including discussion, this film could well project the study into future tasks for religion.

The Work of My Hands. 28 min., color, rental $5.00
   Union of American Hebrew Congregations, 838 Fifth Avenue, New York, N.Y. 10021
What is stewardship? In the story a leader of a Reform Jewish Congregation, which has just built a new synagogue, is reminded through scripture that on many social issues he does not live up to his faith. This film is recommended as an introduction to the study of personal and social religion. Its dramatic elements make it suitable for motivation.

B. Filmstrips

Amos. 27 frames, color, with script, sale $2.50
   United Church Press, United Church of Christ, 1501 Race Street, Philadelphia, Pennsylvania 19102
Amos' indignation at injustice and "surface religion" is examined. The problems which prompted him to speak are presented. Most important, his views on justice in human relations are clearly revealed. This filmstrip is recommended as an introduction to the social religion section of the study. It provides a scriptural and historical base for the readings by Gladden, Wise and Ryan.

Baal Shem Tov—The Teacher of the Grand Word. 66 frames, color, ind. script, sale: $7.50
  Union of American Hebrew Congregations, 838 Fifth Ave., New York, N.Y. 10021
Shows a continuing development of Judaism—particularly of one movement, Hasidism, in the Jewish tradition.

Call for the Question. 53 frame filmstrip, color, sale: $10.00
  Union of American Hebrew Congregations, 838 Fifth Ave., New York, N.Y. 10021
A Negro youth flees into a synagogue for refuge. The rabbi and the elders then face up to the responsibility for social action. (Highly recommended.)

The Challenge of Change. 76 frames, color, with script, sale: $6.00
  Methodist Board of Missions, 475 Riverside Drive, New York, N.Y. 10027
What roles can the churches assume in a time of rapid social change? Questions concerning suburbia, race, urban renewal and population shifts are posed. A discussion, following reading of the social religion material, could then develop around the filmstrip.

II. Articles

"Billy in London," Time, vol. 87 (June 10, 1966).

"Billy Graham's Crusade," Commonweal, vol. 84 (July 22, 1966).

"Christian Faith and Moral Action," Christian Century, vol. 82 (November 3, 1965).

"Church Money for the Slums," America, vol. 119 (November 9, 1968).

"Faith and Experience," Catholic World, vol. 208 (August, 1967).

"Faith or Works?", Catholic World, vol. 205 (August, 1967).

"In Defense of Violence," Time, vol. 91 (November 15, 1968).

"Just What Is the Salvation Army?", Good Housekeeping, vol. 162 (March, 1966).

"Ministering to the Jobless," Christianity Today, vol. 12 (July 19, 1968).

"Nature of Faith," Christianity Today, vol. 12 (November 8, 1968).

"New Shape of the Y," Newsweek, vol. 68 (July 11, 1966).

"92nd Street's 90th [YMHA, YWHA]," Time, vol. 83 (April 10, 1964).

"Several Worlds of American Jews," Harpers, vol. 232 (April, 1966).

"Teens Talk About Religion," Seventeen, vol. 26 (April, 1967).

"Voice for the Poor," America, vol. 118 (February 24, 1968).

"YWCA International Success Story," National Geographic Magazine, vol. 124 (December, 1963).

III. Books

Allport, Gordon. <u>The Individual and His Religion</u>. New York: Macmillan. (paper) $1.50
   A good introduction to the psychological dimension of religion.

Berger, Peter L. <u>The Sacred Canopy: Elements of a Sociological Theory of Religion</u>. Garden City, N.Y.: Doubleday (Anchor Books) (paper) $1.45

Buber, Martin. <u>The Origin and Meaning of Hasidism</u>. New York: Harper and Row, Publishers.

Carmel, Abraham. <u>So Strange My Path</u>. New York: Bloch. $4.95
   Autobiography of conversion to Judaism.

Collier, Richard. <u>General Next to God: Story of William Booth and the Salvation Army</u>. New York: Dutton. $5.50

Merton, Thomas. <u>The Seven Storey Mountain</u>. New York: New American Library. (paper) $.95
   Autobiography of conversion to contemplative Catholicism.

Pollock, John. <u>Billy Graham: The Authorized Biography</u>. Grand Rapids, Michigan: Zondervan. (paper) $.95

St. John, Robert. <u>Jews, Justice and Judaism</u>. Garden City, N.Y.: Doubleday. $6.95

Vorspan, Albert. <u>Jewish Values and Social Crisis: A Casebook for Social Action</u>. Rev. ed. New York: Union of American Hebrew Congregations. (loose-leaf) $4.75

Weisbord, Marvin R. <u>Some Form of Peace</u>. New York: Viking Press $5.95
   The Quaker efforts on behalf of peace.

(In the Basic Library, particular attention is called to the following volumes:

   Abell, <u>American Catholicism and Social Action</u>

   Goldman, <u>Giants of Faith</u>

   McLoughlin, <u>Modern Revivalism</u>

   Stark and Glock, <u>American Piety</u>

   Stedman, <u>Religion and Politics in America</u>)

8
WAYS OF UNDERSTANDING: SCIENCE AND RELIGION

THE PLAN OF THE STUDY

Approaches to Nature

Science and Religion "at War"

Christians Disagree on Darwin

Darwin, the Courts, and the Schools

The Bible and Evolution

Contemporary Parallels

Suggested Activities

Vocabulary

Resource Guide

THE FOCUS OF THIS STUDY

In this Study students are introduced to the idea that religion and science provide us with different ways of understanding. The search for an explanation of nature or the meaning of life is, in turn, rewarded by the unique approaches of science and religion. These unique approaches, and the apparent conflicts in goals and methods, represent seemingly divergent "ways of knowing." In Western civilization, the conflict between these routes to "reliable" knowledge is an enduring issue—feeling, fantasy, the emotions, and faith, on the one hand, and objectivity and reason, on the other. This Study focuses upon one manifestation of this issue, the controversy over evolution, and the "contemporary parallel" section of this Guide offers other topics for class discussion and research. After students have carefully examined the historical controversy about evolution, they should have the opportunity to work more independently upon the contemporary topics—thus, testing their new knowledge and skills through inquiry on additional situations.

THE OBJECTIVES OF THIS STUDY

Knowledge Objectives—Each student will demonstrate his knowledge that:

1. Religion and science each provide "ways of understanding" phenomena.

2. Religion and science reflect different attitudes, goals, methods, and language in examining phenomena and reporting ideas, and both seek "reliable" knowledge for various human aspirations.

3. Darwin's theory of evolution engendered the sharpest conflict between science and religion in America, and the controversy over evolution spread beyond the church into legislative halls, courtrooms, and classrooms.

4. Biblical material has shaped understanding in both scientific and religious realms.

5. The conflicts between religion and science, reason and emotion, feeling and "objective" facts have been enduring issues in Western civilization as men sought to define their commitments and to fulfill their aspirations.

6. While the controversy centering upon evolution continues with diminished intensity, the basic question concerning "ways of understanding" is a contemporary one reflected in current discussions of appropriate life styles, alternative commitments, and reliable knowledge.

Skill Objectives—Each student will demonstrate his ability to:

1. Analyze the nature of argumentation on the "ways of understanding" issues, in terms of value conflicts, assumptions, attempts to persuade, warranting principles, and the styles of grounding conclusions reached.

2. Gather information from highly emotional writing, relevant to analytical questions posed in the Study and by one's self.

3. Compare and contrast authors' positions on an issue in order to generalize about those positions and about the issue under examination.

Value and Attitude Objectives—Each student will demonstrate his willingness to:

1. Examine various positions relative to an issue under study, carefully weighing these alternative positions and the reasons used to back them.

2. Tolerate ambiguity in the resolution of the religion-science conflict, rather than achieving closure by disregarding evidence and conflicting reasons or by rigidly adhering to a position without attending to alternatives.

3. Respect the sensitiveness of others concerning religious issues and beliefs.

APPROACHES TO NATURE

Initially, to impress upon students the different attitudes toward nature, have the two comments on the sun and stars read aloud in class. (Make sure that the oral reader can interpret, by phrasing and inflection, the authors' vastly different perceptions of the heavens.) A short discussion should follow in which students can express their reactions to each comment. They may note different purposes in writing, the orientation of the writers, and the language used by the writers. You might ask: How does each of these comments contribute to one's understanding of the heavens and of nature (or Nature)?

SCIENCE AND RELIGION "AT WAR"; CHRISTIANS DISAGREE ON DARWIN

To illustrate the conflict of religion and science in the American heritage, the Darwinian controversy is presented here. This was, as is related in the student materials, the most serious clash of this nature in America. It should be kept in mind that a conflict between Darwin's theory and biblical teaching is still seen by many Americans today. Therefore, it is imperative that the conscience of each student be respected.

No attempt should be made to judge the wisdom of personal religious beliefs or the validity of scientific theory. The plan of this lesson is to have students objectively study aspects of the controversy, thus illuminating for them the nature of the historical conflict of religion and science. The readings are designed not to produce right or wrong answers, but to cause students to think critically about an area too often clouded by emotion and dogmatism. Science, no less than religion, can be dogmatic; religion, no less than science, can be intelligent. Accordingly, as each reading is discussed, emphasis should be placed upon determining just what the writer is saying regarding evolution theory, how well he says it, and how this differs from what others say. The belief system of the writer is of concern here only as it accounts for what he is saying.

1. For Hodge, what was the evidence that there is design in nature?

The laws of heredity reveal intelligence. Germ cells, for example, show the adaptation of means to a preconceived end. All germ cells are indistinguishable, yet they infallibly develop into one species or another. Why doesn't a germ cell of a fish develop into a bird? (It is exactly like a bird's germ cell!) It is because there is a plan or design behind the process of heredity.

2. What are consequences of a denial of design in nature?

Denial of design in nature results, says Hodge, in a denial of the existence of God.

3. What effect did the theory of evolution have on Abbott's belief?

Abbott's faith is, he says, reinforced rather than threatened by the evolution theory.

4. What was Abbott's main reason for believing evolution to be true?

Evolution is a scientific problem, not a religious one. Abbott bows to the scientists in their area of competence. He had already concluded the Bible was not authoritative on scientific matters. (You may suggest the class speculate on the effect which the age difference between Hodge and Abbott might have on their positions.)[1]

DARWIN, THE COURTS, AND THE SCHOOLS

The importance of the Darwinian controversy in America is further revealed in its political and educational side issues. These issues were of immediate and vital concern to millions of Americans. Basic beliefs were being challenged and basic institutions tested.

In the dying days of the controversy's national prominence, its single most famous (and unfortunately spectacular) event took place. The 1925 Scopes Trial is an example of the political, legal, and educational eruptions caused by an originally religious concern. That religion does not function independently of other elements of society is graphically illustrated here.

---

[1] If you find the thought of these two men of special interest, you may also wish to read a noted American classic: The Education of Henry Adams, Houghton Mifflin, $2.65. Caught up by Social Darwinism as a young man, Henry Adams struggled all his life with the question of design in nature.

THE BIBLE AND EVOLUTION

The "use" of the Bible as a source of learning is further explored here. Bryan and Fosdick present different views of how the Bible is to be used. They are both men who respect and cherish the Bible; yet, each would apply its teaching in a quite dissimilar manner.

1. For Bryan the Bible's authority is to be applied to what areas of life or of learning?

Bryan would really look to the Bible for teaching in all areas of human activity. Here he especially defends the Bible as a source of teaching in science.

2. For Fosdick, in what areas of the Bible is teaching most needed?

Fosdick emphasizes the Bible's value in teaching one how to live. He notes spiritual guidance, inspiration, and principles of living.

3. How, says Fosdick, does Bryan degrade the Bible?

By using the Bible in a way in which it was never meant to be used, says Fosdick, Bryan does a gross injustice to it. By praising it in such an extravagant way, he is in fact holding it up for ridicule.

4. Which argument seems better set forth? Why? Note strengths or weaknesses in each.

Some important points in evaluating the arguments are:

(From Bryan)
"The Bible not only describes man's creation, but gives a purpose for it."
"Evolution does not explain creation."
". . . let them frankly point out . . ."
"Darwinists . . . raise doubt as to future life . . . "

(From Fosdick)
". . . if the Bible is authoritative in biology, then why not in astronomy . . ."
"A denial that the earth moves around the sun . . ."
"Is a cello being defended . . .?"
"Origins prove nothing in the realm of values."

Bryan notes both the inadequacy and invalidity of the Theory of Evolution. It is true that evolution neither explained creation nor provided a purpose for it. Bryan's charge that evolution theory is wrong because it contradicts the Bible would appeal especially to those who found the Bible authoritative in the realm of science.

Fosdick illustrates the folly of using the Bible as a science text by reviving the Copernicus case. In Fosdick's theology, too, the process of creation is rather unimportant. His condemnation of Bryan's misuse of the Bible would appeal especially to those who found the sources for scientific truth outside of Scripture.

CONTEMPORARY PARALLEL

An appropriate follow-up for this study would be an investigation of the events in Arkansas during the 1960's relating to laws against teaching evolution. Another assignment would be to examine current Roman Catholic opinion regarding evolution. Students should also explore other contemporary conflicts that exist between science and religion. The area of morals and medicine raises many such issues: contraception, artificial insemination, sterilization, euthanasia, and organ transplants. One of the most awesome aspects of man's potential "evolution" is in the area of genetic control. Ethicists are deeply concerned about the moral and religious implications of genetic control, and students will find a wealth of material available on this subject. The Reader's Guide would be a good source for such information.

Since the focus of this study is on the basic question of different "ways of knowing," teachers might experiment with introducing students to the current debate between the way of knowing with the mind (cognitive) and the way of knowing with the emotions (enactive). Theologian Sam Keen has captured this conflict in a winsome way that should appeal to students:

> Long ago, when I wore short pants and shot marbles with my left hand, I formed an impression of education which has recently returned to haunt me. Mrs. Jones' first-grade classroom always seemed dark, but on this particular day it was more depressing than usual. For an eternal afternoon I sat practicing my penmanship exercises, listening to Mrs. Jones; monotone: "Make your i's come all the way up to the middle line. And don't forget to make your o's nice and round. Circle, circle, circle. Period. Now repeat." Caught somewhere between boredom and despair I struggled against tears and settled in to wait for the ressurection—the 3:00 o'clock bell.
>
> And then it happened. A movement in a tree outside the window caught my eye and there, in the sweet and redeeming light of the springtime world, was a summer warbler building a nest. Caught in wonder I followed the progress of the nest construction and dreamt of the time when I would be a great ornothologist. My i's and o's were forgotten until Mrs. Jones materialized over my shoulder and demanded to know why three lines in my penmanship book were empty. . . .
>
> It is not surprising that when I finally left the classroom I could dot my i's and make my o's round. But the warbler was gone. I emerged from graduate school to discover that I was empty of enthusiasm. I had a profession but nothing to profess, knowledge but no wisdom, ideas but few feelings. . . . As I shifted my vocation from being a student concerned with possessing and organizing ideas to being a man in search of the wisdom necessary for living with vividness, I came to focus on questions I had not been trained to consider, to cherish abilities which had not been cultivated, and to explore feelings which had long remained dormant. Now, finally, after too many years, I have found my tongue and am talking back to Mrs. Jones.[1]

A number of educators are also "talking back to Mrs. Jones." George Leonard, in his book, Education and Ecstasy (New York: Delacorte Press, 1968), argues that in A.D. 2000 educating the emotions will be accepted as just as important as educating the mind. In Fantasy and Feeling in Education (New York: New York University Press, 1968), Richard Jones criticizes what he sees as an overemphasis on the cognitive aspect of learning in the views of Jerome Bruner. Theodore Roszak in The Making of a Counter Culture (Garden City, New York: Doubleday & Company, Inc., 1969), suggests that a culture which subordinates or degrades visionary experience commits the sin of diminishing our existence. What might be the religious implications in this new emphasis on emotions, feelings, the senses, fantasy, and vision?

---

[1] Sam Keen, To A Dancing God (New York: Harper & Row, Publishers, 1970), pp. 38–40.

SUGGESTED ACTIVITIES

1. Essay

    Write a brief opinion essay in which you seek to answer the following questions:

    a. Why do conflicts between religion and science arise?

    b. How should such conflicts be settled?

    Students should be directed back to the beginning of this lesson. Emphasis should be placed on "ways of understanding." Different attitudes, methods, and languages make science and religion vastly different as techniques. Many have failed to recognize this difference. When people assumed that science and religion had the same goals, conflict between partisans of each was inevitable. Additionally, when one group feels its position or well-being to be endangered by the success of the other, antagonisms are magnified.

    Students should be encouraged to explore any possible ways of settling this conflict. It may be suggested by some students that a certain measure of conflict is desirable. This, too, should be explored.

    On the other hand, is it possible that both science and religion have much in common: namely, a search for meaning? Underneath their obvious divergence, is there a profounder unity? Do some scientists really bow before a transcendant Nature? Do some religionists really worship only the work of men's hands? These are large questions, of course, and students should not be led too far beyond their levels of competence.

Suggestions for Further Research

These areas of investigation are suggested for those students wishing to do additional research. In guiding students in their individual efforts, be sure to use the "Basic Library" as well as the Resource Guide below.

   a. What contemporary conflicts exist between science and religion?

   b. What events in Arkansas during the 1960's relate to laws against teaching evolution?

   c. Investigate current Roman Catholic opinion regarding evolution.

VOCABULARY

academic freedom	epidemic	infallible	rudimentary
authoritative	evolve	intuition	species
benevolent	exploit	perception	spectroscope
contender	fundamental	perplexities	sufficient
depraved	gravitation	predisposition	virtually
eon	indoctrination	prose	virtuous

RESOURCE GUIDE FOR STUDY 8

I. Audio Visual Aids

A. Films

Clay, or the Origin of Species. b&w, rental: apply
United Church of Christ Office for Audio Visuals, 1501 Race St., Philadelphia, Pa. 19102
A satire on the evolutionary history of man. There are no players, just a piece of clay that squirms, twists, and spreads, assuming all kinds of shapes. This film could be well used for motivation.

Creation According to Genesis. 10 min., color, rental $4.00
Produced by H. Boxer, 1949. Available from many denominational and educational film libraries. The story of creation from Genesis 1:1-2:3 is presented in a poetic interpretation by the use of color film, unusual camera effects, editing, and time-lapse photography. The symbolic nature of the story is suggested by showing plants and animals in their full-grown state and by presenting man with footprints and shadows. This film could be shown after students read Section I, "Approaches to Nature."

Darwin and Evolution. 29 min., color, rental $8.20
McGraw-Hill (Text-film department), 330 W. 42nd St., New York, N.Y. 10036
The life and work of Charles Darwin, from his student days to his full maturity as a scientist. The student gains a clearer insight into the theory of evolution and of science, itself.

Monkey Business. 50 min., color, rental $20.00
Gospel films, Box 455, Muskegon, Mich. 49443
Three teen-age boys represent different points of view on the Bible versus Darwin's theory of evolution. One is an agnostic while another believes in the Bible, but he has no intellectual basis for his faith. The third is willing to maintain an open mind and to make his choice from the facts presented. This film proceeds from a conservative theological position, and should be seen as representing a specific religious tradition.

Origin of Life. 29 min., color, rental $8.20
McGraw-Hill (Text-film Dept.), 330 W. 42nd St., New York, N.Y. 10009
This film traces the history of man's various theories on the origin of life. Modern theories are vividly shown and explained.

Overture. color, rental $12.50
Contemporary Films, 267 West 25th St., New York, N.Y. 10001
The development of a chick embryo and its culmination in the hatching of a baby chicken are beautifully shown through the use of color x-ray camera technique. Beethoven's Egmont Overture serves as background music for this film testimony to the marvel of the beginning of life. This film could either initiate or culminate the study.

Patterns of Mind. 22 min., b&w, rental $10.00
Mass Media Ministries, 2116 North Charles St., Baltimore, Maryland 21218
A preview of the exciting world of tomorrow, in which science and religion must cooperate to find answers and workable adaptations. In this film prepared for use with the new curriculum of the Lutheran Church in America, a Christian educator interviews four experts in the fields of astrophysics, political science, computer science, and molecular biology, and obtains their opinions on trends and future developments in their fields.

Science. 29 min., b&w, rental $8.00
   United Church of Christ, 1501 Race St., Philadelphia, Pennsylvania 19102
Discussing the area of science, Dr. Roger Shinn emphasizes that science gives knowledge, and this knowledge then gives power, communication and other elements. Dr. Shinn interviews two scientists who work on new scientific projects and relates how present scientific discoveries are only the beginning of many more to come. They discuss change in the world today and the place of scientific investigation in the world.

Sermon from Science Series
   Moody Bible Institute (Moody Institute of Science) 12000 E. Washington Blvd., Whittier, California 90606
A series of 15 films offering a particular and consistent viewpoint of the relationship of religion and science. The discoveries of science are seen as the discoveries of God's handiwork. These films are an example of one type of religious approach to the relationship of religion and science. Individual titles especially pertinent to this study are:

   City of Bees. 28 min., rental $17.50
   Looks at the pattern and order of social behavior as provided by God.

   Dust on Destiny. 28 min., rental $15.00
   Points out the wonders of man, animals and plants and God's role behind all this.

   Facts of Faith. 37 min., rental $15.00
   Explores the relationship of physical and spiritual forces and what science and the Bible tell us about these forces.

   God of Creation. 28 min., rental $15.00
   Illustrates God's powers in creation.

   The Prior Claim. 28 min., rental $15.00
   God's original plan of creation is shown in science.

B. Filmstrips

   Beginning with God. 49 frame filmstrip, color, cost: $3.50
      Lutheran Church in America, 2900 Queen Lane, Philadelphia, Pennsylvania 19129
   This filmstrip presents the story of Creation in the light of today's scientific knowledge, carefully relating this knowledge to an understanding of God as creator and sustainer of the universe.

   Modern Science and the Christian Faith. Four filmstrips, color, scripts, guides, one 33 1/3 rpm recording. Sale: individual filmstrip, $6.00; record for set of four filmstrips, $5.00, complete set, $24.50   Society for Visual Education, 1345 Diversey Pkwy., Chicago, Illinois 60614

   Science and Religion. 25 frames, introduces viewers to the relation of science and religion pointing out that science discovers what is, not what should be. Through science, atomic energy was discovered, and this force was used to destroy two Japanese cities. Christianity can deal with ethical problems and can complement science by pointing out the uses to which scientific discoveries should be put.

   Religion and Evolution. 25 frames, deals with the relationship between the Biblical understanding of creation and the scientific theory of evolution. It points out differences in conception of time, showing that God created the universe and man over a long period of time.

Technology and Christianity. 24 frames, focuses on the apparent conflict between the demands of a technological age and the responsibilities of faith.

God and Outer Space. 29 frames, discusses the significance of the Christian faith in relation to current scientific discoveries. In dealing with space explorations, the filmstrip emphasizes that God is the God of the whole universe and that Christ's redemption is for all God's creatures. It raises questions concerning our relation to other persons on earth and to God as well as to persons who may be found living on other planets.

The first and second filmstrips in this set are especially recommended. The first could culminate the study; the second could supplement the readings prior to class discussion.

II. Articles

"Churches and Evolution," Christian Century, vol. 84 (May 17, 1967).

"Evolution Revolution in Arkansas," Life, vol. 65 (November 22, 1968).

"Fresh Look at Man: Excerpt from Telihard de Chardin and the Mystery of Christ," Saturday Review, vol. 49 (February 26, 1966).
A Roman Catholic priest and his controversial theory of evolution.

"Great Monkey Trial," New York Times Magazine (July 4, 1965).

"Is the Church Powerless in a Scientific World?" Redbook, vol. 129 (July, 1967).

"J. T. Scopes Redivivus," Christian Century, vol. 84 (April 5, 1967).

"Loneliest Jews of All," Commentary, vol. 46 (August, 1968).

"Making Darwin Legal; U.S. Supreme Court Rules Arkansas Law Unconstitutional," Time, vol. 92 (November 22, 1968).

"Monkeys, Titans and Soda Pop: Scopes Trial," Sr. Scholastic, vol. 90 (May 5, 1967).

"Priest Who Haunts the Catholic World," Saturday Evening Post, vol. 109 (December 21, 1963).
Article on Teilhard de Chardin and his evolutionary theory.

"Science and Christianity," Christianity Today, vol. 12 (August 16, 1968; August 30, 1968).

"Science and Contemporary Theology," Bulletin of Atomic Scientists, vol. 22 (March, 1966).

"Science and the Scriptural View of the Universe," Catholic World, vol. 202 (January, 1966).

"Tennessee Evolution Controversy, After Scopes," Science, vol. 150 (October 22, 1965).

"What Modern Science Offers the Church," Saturday Review, vol. 49 (November 19, 1966).

"Where Religion and Science Meet," Saturday Review, vol. 46 (March 23, 1965).

III. Books

De Camp, L. Sprague. The Great Monkey Trial, Garden City, N.Y.: Doubleday $7.95
This is the latest and the best treatment of the Scopes trial.

Lawrence, Jerome, and Lee, Robert E. Inherit the Wind. Bantam. (paper) $0.50

Morrison, John L. A History of American Catholic Opinion on the Theory of Evolution 1859-1950. Available: University Microfilms, Ann Arbor, Michigan.

Scopes, John T. and Presley, James. Center of the Storm: Memoirs of John T. Scopes. New York: Holt, Rinehart and Winston. $5.95

White, Andrew D. History of the Warfare of Science with Theology in Christendom. New York: Free Press (paper) $2.95

9

CONSCIENCE OR CONSTITUTION

THE PLAN OF THE STUDY

A Matter of Conscience

The Mormons and Polygamy

Jehovah's Witnesses and the Flag

Contemporary Parallel

Suggested Activities

Vocabulary

Resource Guide

THE FOCUS OF THIS STUDY

In this study students are directed to that uniquely human quality called <u>conscience</u>. Conscience, its nature, its source, its development, has commanded the attention of men both within and without the religious community. Successful social living in less than a completely authoritarian environment demands that members of the group possess conscience in some measure. In a democracy where individuals are entrusted with both decision-making responsibilities and a certain amount of "self-policing," commitment to conscience is even more vital. However, the very nature of our democratic and pluralistic society makes a required conformity of conscience unacceptable. Yet, group harmony is necessary for group survival. It is within the framework of such conscience conflict that this study proceeds.

THE OBJECTIVES FOR THIS STUDY

<u>Knowledge Objectives</u>—Each student will demonstrate his knowledge that:

1. Conscience is that mental faculty which provides an awareness of what is moral, good, or right and a feeling of obligation to live in accordance with that awareness.

2. Conscience is respected in our society as a supreme human quality.

3. Conscience derives its authority, as it resides in each individual, from various sources which according to the individual may lend greater or lesser authority to his conscience.

4. Religion-based conscience and the social behavior dictated by conscience have tested the constitutional reconciliation of liberty and authority.

5. While government under our laws may concern itself with religious practice, it may not impose religious belief.

Skill Objectives—Each student will demonstrate his ability to:

1. Define the meaning of concepts as used in context by various authors.

2. Extract information from materials which treat religion in a rational, legal, and historical perspective.

3. Interpret various definitions of conscience as found in literary and historical sources.

4. Generalize about the relationship of conscience to human behavior, and about the relationship of liberty to authority in our society.

5. Analyze decisions based upon warrants and grounding, assumptions made, projection of consequences as to their validity, and evaluation of consequences based upon value analysis.

Value and Attitude Objectives—Each student will demonstrate his willingness to:

1. Explore the relevancy of issues of conscience in one's own life, and the behavior that specific situations might elicit given his values and commitments.

2. Attend to, and empathize with, the conscience-obligations of others in specific conflict situations, even if these obligations are perceived as being quite different from one's own.

3. Express commitment to the fundamental principle of American civil and religious liberty—the freedom and dignity of each individual personality.

A MATTER OF CONSCIENCE

Being Conscious of Conscience

These passages are designed to introduce conscience within a framework familiar to students. Some passages will have more appeal than others. Students may wish to comment on or discuss the passages; however, no structured discussion is planned as the readings are intended to introduce and stimulate thinking about conscience. Have students read this section in class and then go on to the next section.

The Quality Called Conscience

Five Views of Conscience

Conscience is not easy to define. It means much to some, little to others. To illustrate this, five quotations have been presented to students. Class discussion of the quotations should emphasize the variety of "definitions" of conscience.

The sections The Nature of Conscience, The Use of Conscience, and A Conflict of Conscience set the stage for the main part of the study. You may wish to clarify points in discussion.

THE MORMONS AND POLYGAMY

Questions are designed to guide students through the reading. Though they are not intended for class discussion, you may wish to go over them in class after students have finished the reading assignment. In this way, student comprehension of the material can be determined.

1. What did the Court decide?

The Court decided that the statute against bigamy was within the legislative power of Congress--that it was a constitutional law.

2. What chain of reasoning does the Justice use in arriving at this conclusion?

The law is valid and constitutional as it does not violate the First Amendment. The law is made to govern actions. Individuals are not exempt from the law even when they call their actions religious. Thus, the Mormon is guilty.

3. What information does the Justice supply to support the claim that the law in question is valid?

Polygamy has for centuries been prohibited in Western civilization. It has been treated as an offense against society in the West and has always been an offense in the United States. Marriage is a civil contract regulated by law in most civilized nations.

4. What examples of behavior does the Justice use to illustrate his contention that denial of practice of religion is valid? Why might he choose these particular examples?

Human sacrifices as part of religious worship and the wife burning herself to death as the husband is cremated are spectacular and repulsive examples and thus should win support for the judge's argument since he treats polygamy as a parallel.

5. What does the Justice imply would happen to society if the Mormons were allowed to follow their conscience? Does this prediction seem valid?

Law and order would disappear as each man, following his religious beliefs, would become a law unto himself. Thus, the Justice defends his conclusion on the grounds that the absence of this law would lead to an undesirable consequence. Students might examine this to see if the prediction of such a consequence is warranted.

JEHOVAH'S WITNESSES AND SALUTING THE FLAG

1. In the Gobitis case, what does Justice Frankfurter feel to be the most important concern?

Society has the right to use the educational process to create a unifying sentiment and thus preserve society (and the liberties of the people).

2. How does Justice Stone disagree with the majority opinion? What arguments does he use?

Though he agrees that government may teach patriotism and love of country, he disagrees that government may compel an individual to swear allegiance to that which he does not believe, that is, to bear false witness (to his religion). The justice argues that the individual must be free from compulsion as to what he shall think and what he shall say. The state has no authority to compel belief or the expression of it. He notes that there are other ways to teach loyalty—ways better than compulsory expression of belief.

3. In the Barnette Case, what is the greatest danger foreseen, by Justice Jackson, if activities such as the flag salute are made compulsory?

As moderate efforts to compel people to think or behave uniformly fail, harsher measures are taken. This results in greater strife and diversion rather than in unity of sentiment. Ultimately, dissenters are eliminated in order to achieve unity of opinion or belief.

4. How has Justice Frankfurter's emphasis changed in writing his Barnette decision as compared to Gobitis?

In the Barnette Case, Frankfurter emphasizes that the flag salute is not a violation of freedom of conscience, as people may still believe what they want. In Gobitis, his emphasis was on the legitimacy of the salute as an educational process for the good of society.

CONTEMPORARY PARALLEL

For this study students will want to investigate some of the "conscience or constitution" issues since 1940. Perhaps the most significant cases are those that relate to conscientious objectors. Two important Supreme Court cases deserve careful study in this area. A report on the case of U.S. v. Seeger (1965) would make an excellent assignment. In this case, Daniel Seeger, a young pacifist and humanist, had been denied conscientious objector classification on the ground that he had checked neither "Yes" nor "No" on the question of belief in a Supreme Being (appearing on Form 150, the special c.o. form) and had affirmed "belief in the devotion to goodness and virtue for their own sakes and a religious faith in a purely ethical creed . . . without belief in God, except in the remotest sense . . . the cosmic order does, perhaps, suggest a creative intelligence. . . ." The Court gave Seeger c.o. classification, with Justice Clark declaring, "We believe . . . the test of belief in relation to a Supreme Being is whether a given belief that is sincere and meaningful occupies a place in the life of its possessor parallel to that filled by the orthodox belief in God of one who clearly qualifies for the exemption." The other case is the 1970 decision of the Supreme Court against "selective" objection to war.

Another interesting area for this study is the matter of loyalty oaths. What were the arguments of the Supreme Court's 1971 decision rejecting part of Florida's loyalty oath for state employees? Other areas for research reports include abortion laws, Sunday closing laws, blood transfusions, the LSD cult, union shop regulations, capital punishment, and religious exercise in public schools.

SUGGESTED ACTIVITIES

1. Written Assignment

   a. In a short essay defend or attack the following statement (examine closely the opinions of Justices Waite and Stone for supporting evidence):

   Even though Justice Stone disagreed with the majority in the Gobitis Case (1940), he would probably have agreed with the majority in the Reynolds Case (1879) had he heard the case then.

   (While the construction of "what if" speculations by removing people and events from their proper historical contexts poses some problems, illuminating comparisons and contrasts may be seen. Thus the emphasis in this activity should be placed upon "process" not results.)

   The social context in which judicial decisions are made can never be ignored if one wishes to account for all variables in ascertaining a relationship between events. Regarding the social context, it might be noted that in 1879, the Court reflected less libertarian views than we expect from it today. America, though rapidly becoming more diverse with each new wave of immigration, was not the pluralistic society we know today. The validity of traditionally held values was not subject to question as it is in the present. Justice Stone's decision would reflect thinking more in tune with the social milieu of 1879 than 1940.

Even if we could transport Justice Stone and his 1940 thinking back to 1879, there is reason to believe he would still have voted with the majority. This can be concluded from an examination of his 1940 opinion and the issues in the Reynolds Case. The 1879 case involved a religious practice seen as dangerous to the general welfare of the people. It did not involve, as did the 1940 Gobitis Case, the confession of belief. In 1879 Justice Waite stated that while laws cannot interfere with religious belief, they may with practice. In 1940 Justice Stone shows agreement when he said that "government may suppress religious practices dangerous to morals, and presumably those also which are dangerous to public safety, health, and good order." Of course, it is possible to argue that Justice Stone might not have viewed polygamy as dangerous to society and that he, therefore, would have voted as he did in the Gobitis Case.

b. In a one-page paper explain whether the following quotation would be a compliment to or a criticism of the Jehovah's Witnesses in 1940 and the Mormons in 1879:

"The nonconformist conscience makes cowards of us all."
—Sir Max Beerbohm, King Richard the Fourth

Students may experience much difficulty in interpreting this subtle statement on conscience. Care should be taken to make its meaning clear to all. This is especially important in light of contemporary developments concerning civil disobedience, anti-establishment crusades, youth rebellion and the widespread challenging of traditional institutions. Beerbohm is arguing that conscience-born nonconformity demands more courage and fortitude than the "easy-out" of conformity. Though Madison Avenue cliches of the "dare to be different" variety abound, conformity is still the byword of safety and security. The supposed nonconformity of outlandish attire and convention-flouting behavior is but conformity of a different sort. One must look hard for any trace of conscience here. When one turns, however, to the behaviors of the Jehovah's Witnesses, the Amish, or others attempting to remain true to their beliefs in the face of ridicule, scorn and hardship, one may come closer to the nonconformist conscience of which Beerbohm speaks. Or, do these groups only have different "conformities"? The cowards are, of course, those who deny their conscience or who neglect to face directly the issues that a sensitive conscience might raise. Present-day American value orientations, emphasizing sociability, group-orientation, other-directedness, well-roundedness and committee-thinking, tend to reject individualistic nonconformity.

Conformity, students should understand, is not bad per se. What is bad, implies Beerbohm, is the cowardice of those who fail to follow their conscience—what they believe in—because in the social setting it is easier not to follow it.

c. In 1651, Roger Williams of Rhode Island wrote to Governor John Endecott of Massachusetts to protest the whipping of a Baptist. "Be pleased then, honored Sir, to know that that thing which we call conscience is of such a nature as once a Pope of Rome himself observed that although it be groundless, false and deluded—yet it is not by any arguments or torments easily removed."

Choose one of the following:

1. Write an autobiographical paper in which you support Roger Williams' declaration by by using as an example a belief or act of conscience held or felt by you. Tell why it would "not by any arguments or torments [be] easily removed."

2. Write an account (factual or fictional) of an individual's behavior which would support Roger Williams' declaration. Describe the belief or act of conscience and why the individual holds it.

The primary objective of this activity is to help students develop a profound respect for conscientiousness in themselves or in others. Possessing the courage to follow conscience when one knows this will be burdensome, unrewarding, or even painful is a gift given to few. In an age characterized by the cool, the detached and the noncommitted, the worthy commitments of individuals are seldom reinforced by praise.

Students should be encouraged to try to write the autobiographical paper (a). However, some may be embarrassed by this assignment. Thus, alternative (b) is provided particularly for these students.

Suggestions for Further Research

These areas of investigation are suggested for those students wishing to do additional research. In guiding students in their individual efforts, be sure to use the "Basic Library" as well as the Resource Guide below.

a. In our own day, conscience-constitution tensions are most evident in connection with selective service laws.

1. From recent newspapers and magazines, describe at least three instances involving conscientious objection to military service. Were all objections on "religious" grounds? How were the cases handled? What was the public reaction?

2. What can you learn about the history of conscientious objection in this country? When did it begin? What laws were passed to deal with it?

3. Study any one religious group in America which has historically been a "peace" church. What arguments are offered on behalf of their position? What counter-arguments can be made?

b. Study the case of Pierce v. Society of Sisters which came before the United States Supreme Court in 1925. What was the issue of conscience here? How was the case resolved? Explain your reasons for agreeing or disagreeing with the decision.

VOCABULARY

common law	idolatry	oblivion	sovereignty
convictions	infallibility	petty	sphere
derided	literal	phenomenon	subordination
dictates	martyrdom	profound	tribulation
dynasty	moral	pyre	valid
guaranty	obligation	sentiment	verities

RESOURCE GUIDE FOR STUDY 9

I. Audio Visual Aids

A. Films

Alternatives. 24 min., color, rental: apply
Produced by National Service Board for Religious Objectors and cooperating agencies. Available from Fellowship of Reconciliation, Nyack, New York
This film explores the legitimate alternatives to military service that are open to conscientious objectors. The legal provisions which safeguard the rights of conscientious objectors are presented. With the discussion guide provided with the film, an additional class discussion could well conclude this study.

Freedom to Learn. 28 min., color or b&w, rental: Free Loan
Produced by National Education Association. Available from Florida Education Association, 208 W. Pensacola St., Tallahassee, Florida 32301
A high school social studies teacher of twenty-five years experience honestly faces a challenge to her personal and professional philosophy. The teacher has a conscientious obligation to open the minds of her students to the totality of knowledge and to urge them to find truth for themselves. For doing so, she is accused of teaching communism. The film could well be used after the class discussions in the Activities section.

I Pledge Allegiance. 24 min., rental $11.50
McGraw-Hill (Text-film Dept.), 330 W. 42nd St., New York, N.Y. 10036
This film explores the concept of loyalty in a democracy and considers examples of the expression of loyalty in wartime. It includes treatment of Benedict Arnold and Robert E. Lee.

The Reynolds Story. 20 min., b&w, rental $3.00
American Friends Service Committee (A-V Dept.), 160 N. 15th St., Philadelphia, Pa. 19102
An anthropologist and his family making moral decision sail their yacht into an area restricted for nuclear testing. They are then arrested and tried. Their Quaker ideals and pacifist beliefs concerning nuclear warfare are well presented. This film illustrates a religion-based conscience guiding human behavior. This film should come after students have read about the Jehovah's Witnesses. The legal case involving the Quakers (Friends) could then be added to the general discussion concerning obedience to higher law.

Right or Wrong. 11 min., color or b&w, rental $2.25
Produced by Coronet Films, 65 E. South Water St., Chicago, Illinois 60601
When some high school boys break a warehouse window, a number of moral decisions must be made. The night watchman, a boy's mother, the property owner, the police sargeant, a social worker, and one of the boys face a moral problem. This film could be used to introduce the study of conscience.

What is Conscience? 11 min., b&w, rental $2.25
Produced by Coronet Films, 65 E. South Water St., Chicago, Illinois 60601
The film explores the many effects of conscience and how each person can use his conscience. Different explanations of conscience are presented and dramatic incidents are used to illustrate the workings of conscience. This film could well supplement part B of section I of this study.

Where the People Are. b&w, rental: Apply
   Inquire to Broadcasting and Film Commission, Film Distribution Dept., 475 Riverside Dr., Room 861, New York, N.Y. 10027
In this film, a conservative 25 year-old seminarian seeks answers to the issue of conscientious objection. This film could be the basis for additional discussion of an issue concerning most high school boys.

Which Way to Peace? 30 min., b&w, rental $7.50
   Produced by The Methodist Church. Available from University of Southern California, Film Distribution Division, University Park, Los Angeles, California 90007
The film presents a discussion-debate between two church leaders, Dr. Henry Hitt Crane and Bishop G. Bromley Oxnam. Each man defends his position on the greater question of peace on the basis of Christian tradition. The film shows how two people can follow their consciences based on religious authority and still be in conflict. This film could supplement the discussion of conflict of conscience.

With Liberty and Justice for All. 55 min., b&w, rental $9.75
   Produced by Ford Foundation and released through McGraw-Hill Text Films, 330 W. 42nd Street, New York, N.Y. 10036
The film discusses the role of the Supreme Court and many of its historic decisions concerning individual rights preserved by the Constitution.

This film would help to place the Mormon and Jehovah's Witness cases in historical perspective. If used, it would best follow the reading on both of these cases.

II. Articles

"Conscience and the Constitution," PTA Magazine, vol. 58 (November 1963).

"Court Abdicates: Flag Salute Case," Christian Century, vol. 57 (July 3, 1940).

"Court Martial of Captain Noyd," Harper, vol. 236 (June, 1968).

"Hershey and the Draft," New Republic, vol. 157 (December 2, 1967).

"Judaism, Israel, and Conscientious Objection." Christian Century, vol. 86 (September 3, 1969).

"Law and Conscience." America, vol. 122 (February 21, 1970).

"Let's Forget the First Amendment," Saturday Evening Post, vol. 240 (June 17, 1969).

"Question of Conscience," Seventeen, vol. 26 (February, 1967).

"Religious Freedom: Flag Salute Case; Complete text of majority opinion and of dissent with editorial comment," New Republic, vol. 102 (June 24, 1940).

"Role of Conscience in the Modern World: Conference under Catholic, Jewish, and Protestant Sponsorship," America, vol. 116 (May 20, 1967).

"Salute to the Court; Jehovah's Witnesses Case," New Republic, vol. 108 (March 1, 1943).

"Who Must Serve: Beliefs and the Draft." Senior Scholastic, vol. 99 (September 14, 1970).

III. Books

Finn, James E. (editor) A Conflict of Loyalties: The Case for Selective Conscientious Objection. Western Publishing Co. (Pegasus) (paper) $1.95

Konvitz, Milton R. Religious Liberty and Conscience: A Constitutional Inquiry. New York: Viking Press (paper) $1.35

Long, Edward L. War and Conscience in America. Philadelphia: Westminster Press (paper) $1.65

(In the Basic Library, particular attention is called to the following volumes:

Cogley, Religion in America

Stokes and Pfeffer, Church and State in the United States

Tussman, The Supreme Court on Church and State

Wilson, Church and State in American History)

10

AMERICA: PROTESTANT OR PLURALIST?

THE PLAN OF THE STUDY

  Introduction

  Protestant Nativism and Roman Catholic Response

  Jews in America

  Eastern Orthodoxy in America

  Patterns of Pluralism

  Problems of Pluralism

  Contemporary Parallel

  Suggested Activities

  Vocabulary

  Resource Guide

THE FOCUS OF THIS STUDY

What is the meaning of pluralism in America? Throughout its history, the United States has been the receiving nation for thousands of migrants, each bringing their customs and religious traditions. The popular notion of America as a "melting pot" which assimilates diverse ethnic groups and casts a united population with common dispositions and aspirations often runs aground when held up to the historical evidence. Many groups have not be so assimilated, and the population has been and continues to be diverse, with people cherishing many of those differences.

This Study focuses upon the nature of pluralism in America, reactions to the plural character of our society, and the desirability of pluralism vis-a-vis other conceptions of society. Specifically, students have an opportunity to inquire into the experiences of three groups: Roman Catholics, Jews, and Eastern Orthodox. And then, examine the patterns of pluralism in America and the problems attending this diversity. In the "contemporary parallel" section, teachers may encourage their students to deal directly with one manifestation of pluralism—the issues attending the treatment of religion in public education.

A NOTE ABOUT ATTITUDES

This Study contains many opportunities for the development of desirable attitudes. As the accounts of the Catholic, Jewish, and Eastern Orthodox experiences are discussed in class, any chance prejudicial comments of students should not be allowed to create an unfavorable atmosphere. In the initial discussion teacher and students can set the proper tone for the complete study. It is quite possible to talk directly to students of proper attitude development all the while fostering undesirable attitudes. Exhortation rarely works. Biases must be altered indirectly, for a direct challenge to a student often results in his retreat and a reinforcement of the bias. Religious and ethnic discrimination can be dealt with rationally. An inquiry into the nature and sources of prejudice can provide students the opportunity to discover for themselves the untenable, inconsistent, and self-contradicting positions they may hold. Above all, attitude development ultimately depends on the attitudes and values projected by the teacher and the teacher's skill in bringing about attitude change.

THE OBJECTIVES FOR THIS STUDY

Knowledge Objectives—Each student will demonstrate his knowledge that:

1. America has changed from a predominantly Protestant nation to a pluralistic one.

2. Immigration has accounted for a large part of this change, and these immigrants in the nineteenth and twentieth centuries encountered problems adjusting to American society, and many Americans experienced problems in adjusting to the presence of diverse ethnic groups and their religious traditions.

3. Some of the immigrants' problems are manifestations of the "unavoidable tension" between religion and secular society.

4. Religious prejudice may include economic, cultural, and political elements.

5. Members of a religious group may disagree on how much accommodation to society or to other religious groups is desirable.

6. Compromise can be more difficult in resolving sacred than secular issues.

7. The openness and pragmatism of American society poses special problems for religion.

8. Acquiescence in discrimination is equal to active discrimination.

Skill Objectives—Each student will demonstrate his ability to:

1. Make inferences from data presented on charts and graphs.

2. Apply the theory of "unavoidable tension" to historical events and contemporary issues.

3. Compare and contrast positions on a religious issue.

4. Define and formulate solutions to problems of religious pluralism, justifying these solutions with reasonable arguments.

Value and Attitude Objectives—Each student will demonstrate his willingness to:

1. Examine various positions on a controversial issue, attending carefully and critically to the grounds offered to support those positions, before forming one's own judgment.

2. Desire the elimination of religious intolerance and prejudice, and the treatment of others as equals.

3. Appreciate the traditions and institutions of America's religious communities.

4. Show empathy for religious leaders who seek an accommodation of religious tradition with new social environment, without compromising basic principles, and empathy for members of religious communities who have faced the pressures of conformity and change while holding on to cherished commitments and beliefs.

INTRODUCTION

The introductory section of this study provides a background and frame of reference for the subsequent assignments. The primary point to be brought home to students is that prior to mid-nineteenth century the United States was very much a Protestant nation, but by mid-twentieth century the nation was decidedly pluralistic with no denomination commanding the allegiance of a majority of the people.

Information in this section is provided in a reading assignment which contains tables and graphs. The primary learning activity is a teacher-led discussion based on these three charts. Discussion should be centered on describing and explaining the trends in the religious affiliation of Americans. Emphasis is placed upon (1) gaining knowledge about the growth of religious traditions in the United States and (2) developing skill in using tables and graphs as sources of information. The discussion should occur after students have read all of the Introduction.

When discussing Table I, the following should be included.

1. Which groups seemed dominant in 1740? 1780? 1820?

In 1740 the Congregational (in New England, primarily) and the Anglican (especially in the South) churches enjoyed favored status in the colonies. By 1780 the Baptist and Presbyterian churches were challenging the Congregationalists' number one position. By 1820 clearly the Baptist and Methodist churches were most numerous, with Presbyterian and Congregational following.

2. Which groups seemed to grow most rapidly?

The most rapid growth rates were those of the Baptists and Methodists. Presbyterians, too, multiplied at a good rate. Lutherans had grown eightfold between 1740 and 1820 while Roman Catholics were over five times as numerous at the end of the 80-year period. Slowest growth rates were experienced by the Dutch and German Reformed Churches, the Congregational and the Anglican (Episcopal) Churches.

3. Offer some possible reasons why one group may grow more rapidly than another?

The Congregational (1620, Massachusetts) and Anglican (1607, Virginia) churches enjoyed a headstart (and official "establishment" in some states) over other churches. However, this advantage had disappeared by 1820. Additionally, the Anglican Church tie with mother England caused it to suffer after the Revolutionary War. Immigration at this time was largely from England, Scotland, and Germany. This can account in part for the Reformed, Lutheran, and Presbyterian growth. The Presbyterians (sometimes in concert with Congregationalists) also engaged in much missionary work. The most effective missionaries, however, were the Baptists and Methodists. They were particularly active on the frontier working among those who settled in the Trans-Appalachian West. Employing novel methods (such as the Methodist "circuit-rider") and preaching a popular Gospel, these churches remained the largest Protestant denominations. Not until after 1820 would Catholic immigration make the Roman church grow rapidly.

After discussing Table I, turn to an examination of Figures 2 and 3.

1. What changes in American society would help account for the sharp rise in both Catholic and Protestant numbers after 1860?

After 1870 with the industrialization of America, the total population enjoyed a faster growth rate. Industrialization also beckoned more immigrants.

2. What might explain the tapering off of the Catholic (but not Protestant) increase during the 1900–1940 period? (Note, too, the similar trend in Jewish growth after 1920.)

Events in Europe—especially World War I—affected the flow of immigrants to the United States. In 1924 restrictive immigration laws were passed. These laws favored immigration from the British Isles and Northern and Western Europe. The laws discriminated against Eastern and Southern Europeans, as well as non-Europeans. In the decade of the 1930's immigration dropped to a level below that of the 1830's.

3. At what point was the Protestant population approximately equal to the 1960 Jewish figure? At what point did Roman Catholicism reach the 1960 Eastern Orthodox figure? What does this tell us about the "arrival times" of these four groups?

In 1865 Protestant membership was just under six millions. By 1960 this was the figure for America's Jews. Eastern Orthodox Americans numbered about three millions in 1960; Roman Catholicism reached that number around 1860. Point out to students how a study of these graphs above could tell us of the sequence of adding Catholic, then Jewish, then Orthodox populations to the once almost exclusively Protestant American population.

4. Note that all four groups have increasing growth rates after 1940. Can you explain this?

Point out to students that the post-1950 growth rate seems to take a sharp upward turn when compared with the post-1920 period. Remember that restrictions were placed on immigration in 1924. Secondly, the depression was accompanied by reduced birth rates. However, after World War II there was renewed immigration, including refugees from War-torn nations. Note, too, the post-war baby boom and the accelerated growth of our own total population. Finally, there was a marked increase in church membership. That is, a greater percentage of Americans (of a larger population) were church members than ever before. (See below.)

5. Find the total population of the United States in 1860; in 1960. (The World Almanac is a good source.) Relate this to Figures 1 and 2. What does this tell us about the attractiveness of church membership to Americans? What percentage of Americans were church members in 1860? in 1960? What might account for this change?

The total population of the United States in 1860 was 31,443,321. In 1960 the population was 179,323,175. The graph tells us that there were approximately seven million church members (Catholic and Protestant) in 1860. Thus approximately 22% of the population were church members in 1860. Adding Catholic, Jewish, Orthodox, and Protestant Church populations shown in Figures 1 and 2 reveals that the total church membership was approximately 54% of the national population in 1960. While the preceding information does not indicate either church involvement or religious commitment it does indicate that the fact of religious pluralism is a major consideration in understanding the nature of American society. With the existence of pluralism now established, we turn to an examination of what pluralism has meant for the development of modern America—what special benefits accrue from religious diversity; what special problems are engendered?

PROTESTANT NATIVISM AND THE ROMAN CATHOLIC RESPONSE

The first large-scale challenge to Protestantism's virtual monopoly on American religious life was a Roman Catholic one. That challenge provoked denials of Catholicisms very worth as a faith for men and attacks upon it as alien to America and offensive to "real" Americans. These anti-Catholic efforts are grouped under the label "nativism." At worst these efforts preceded the hate-mongering of the Ku Klux Klan and American Nazi's. At best they involved learned but fearful men who, often eloquently, argued that America's institutions could stand only upon Protestant foundations. In this part of the study students should come to know (1) the main charges of the Nativists, (2) the sources of those charges, and (3) how Catholics refuted those charges. (Note: Later in the study we shall take up consideration of "unavoidable tension" between religious and secular society. For loyalty to God does transcend loyalty to a secular society. This is a source of tension central to the Nativist controversy. However, you are advised to only touch upon this now, if at all, because additional reading and extended discussion will later focus on this problem.) Information about nativism and Catholic responses is found in four primary source readings. Discussion centered on these readings concludes the first section. The following should be brought out in the discussion.

1. According to the advice of the bishops, how should Catholics react to attacks by Nativists? Was this good advice? Why? Why not? How do you feel Catholics could best answer the false charges leveled against them?

In their pastoral letter the bishops advise Catholics to ignore the attacks. They urge Catholics to continue to act as responsible American citizens. This was good advice. To urge retaliation in kind—which sometimes was the case—would have only fanned the flames of hostility. Instead Catholics, by assuming the responsibilities of democratic citizenship, proved the Nativists wrong. Catholics could be and were good Americans. In fact, their upholding of constitutional liberties while Nativists were, in the name of liberty, actually trampling them earned Catholicism much respect.

2. Which of the four points of Article II of the Constitution of the American Protestant Association do you consider the least defensible as legitimate church goals? Why? Are any defensible? If so, which? Why?

The fourth point, "To awaken the attention of the Community . . . ," would be least acceptable as legitimate goals for a Christian church (or a Jewish synogogue, for that matter). Here the churches were seeking to enlist public energies and community passions in their private fight for religious hegemony. Certainly the goal is not consistent with the basic teachings of these churches. Secondly, the type of civil action implied in the objective is incompatible with basic American ideals and the role of the churches in a secular society. Points one, two, and three of Article II could be legitimate goals though the derogatory language used in the first and third points would make them unacceptable to most Christians. (Note: "Popery" and Romanism were popular terms of derision used by anti-Catholics. In 1884 James G. Blaine, Republican candidate for President called the Democratic Party, "the party of Rum, Romanism, and Rebellion." The large Catholic vote then swung behind underdog Grover Cleveland to help elect him president.)

3. Examine the points used by Josiah Strong to illustrate the claim that Catholicism and the Republic were incompatible.

    a. Which would be easiest to refute?
    b. Which would be most difficult to refute?
    c. Are there any which need no refutation?

Explain your choices.

In discussing the points used by Josiah Strong the following should be considered.

a. The sovereignty of the Pope was not in direct opposition to that of the people. In America, the Pope's sovereignty was real only in religious matters. The people's sovereignty is, of course, a sovereignty in Civil government.

b. The highest allegiance of Catholics was to God, not to temporal laws. So, too, the allegiance of Protestants was to God first. Protestants could put the Bible before the Constitution with clear conscience if conflict of loyalties was perceived. This type of conflict could involve Jews and many groups of Christians, not just Catholics.

c. The Pope, except for those living in the Papal States prior to 1870 and in Vatican City thereafter, was no temporal ruler. Obedience to the Pope in matters of faith was the private concern of Catholics, not the public concern of civil government. This kind of Papal rule did not conflict with allegiance to the United States in temporal matters.

d. In Spain, Italy, and some predominantly Catholic countries intolerance was supported. In other nations where Anglicanism or Lutheranism was established, Catholicism was discriminated against by law. However, in the United States as in some other countries, Catholic leaders advocated tolerance. Intolerance was not a basic article of Catholic faith. It was a basic article of the Nativist faith—and of earlier centuries.

e. Rome retained control over Catholic religious teachings. Thus, she avoided the fragmentation of Protestantism. Also, the Catholic Church, as did Protestant churches, censored literature it deemed harmful to the faithful. Additionally, the Church required its clergy to have approval before issuing new interpretations of ecclesiastic policy or teachings. This does not mean, however, that Catholicism was incompatible with the civil liberties of press and of speech.

f. Establishment as a national church was not an exclusive quality of Roman Catholicism. The Church of England, the Church of Scotland, and Lutheran Churches in various European nations enjoyed established status. Both the Anglican and Congregational churches had such status in the United States until the early nineteenth century. When it was in their best interests, most Protestants supported alliance of church and state as much as Catholics. In America, Catholic support of separation of church and state was added to that of Protestants and Jews.

g. The public school system in America had a Protestant flavor. The King James Bible was read, Protestant prayers were recited, and Sectarian teaching was common. Catholic protests went largely unheeded. This situation led to the development of a parochial school system. Additionally, Catholic leaders felt that worship needed to be reinforced by education—all from a consistent point of view.

All the points may be refuted by the counter charge that they are made up of distortions, half-truths, and vague generalities. Points a, b, and c confuse religious conscience and civic loyalty. All religious believers, as we have noted, hold sacred allegiances which may supersede those of secular state. The Nativists sought to equate this higher loyalty of Catholics with a disloyalty to the United States. When the different realms of these competing loyalties are understood, then Catholics are seen along with all others holding religious commitments that transcend earthly states.

Points d, e, and f should be viewed as partial truths that could apply as well to many Protestant churches. In America Catholics claimed protection under the very laws Nativists were trampling. In Spain, Italy, and Latin America the Church did support undemocratic policies. However, it is improper to regard the whole Catholic Church as of one mind. Its clergy as well as the laity could reflect or adapt to a variety of national patterns and policies. Point g should be considered in light of the Protestant flavor then permeating the public school systems.

4. What is the main theme of Cardinal Gibbons? Is this a good way of opposing the Nativists?

Cardinal Gibbons asserts that American Catholics have found no difficulty harmonizing their duties as citizens with their obligations as Catholics. Certain non-Catholics, however, view such harmony as unobtainable. Therefore they seek to relieve Catholics of their citizenship responsibilities and exclude them from its rewards. The Cardinal points out that anti-Catholics practice the very evils of which they accuse Catholics. They seek to preserve the liberties of all by destroying the liberties of some. Cardinal Gibbons presents the best type of argument to oppose the Nativists: That they by their very actions destroy that which they claim to preserve.

5. What evidence can you find in the four readings that the charges against Catholics had changed little from 1833 to 1909? Are any of these charges leveled at Catholics today?

In 1833, the bishops noted that "they have denounced us as enemies to the liberties of the republic." By associating Protestantism with patriotism, and Catholicism with subversion Nativists sought to frighten some older Americans with loss of their freedoms. Many years later Cardinal Gibbons could still note the Nativist charge ". . . their religion is opposed to American liberties."

Similar charges were hurled at Al Smith, Democratic candidate for President in 1928. They were resurrected in 1960 in a vain attempt to defeat John F. Kennedy. Today, faint rumblings of Nativism can be heard when such issues as federal aid to schools, birth control, and sending an envoy to the Vatican are discussed. These issues may all be vigorously debated, of course, but they should be argued on their own merits and not on the basis of blanket antagonism toward any group or church.

JEWS IN AMERICA

The second large immigrant group of non-Protestants was Jewish. Though the first American Jews arrived when New York was still Dutch New Amsterdam, it wasn't until the nineteenth century that Jews began to contribute significantly to America's emerging pluralism. The Jew in America was confronted with two problems which we examine in this study. One problem was new: Americanization. The other was very old: anti-Semitism.

Since these two problems are not unrelated in the Jew's American experience, they shall be treated together in class discussion. Students should understand that some Jews resisted appeals to Americanize because of age old fears of anti-Semitism. Other Jews resisted for fear of losing a heritage that was sacred and precious. Motivists, meanwhile, adapted time-worn anti-Semitic propaganda to fit the American scene.

Two sets of guiding questions direct students to the significant aspects of each issue. Discussion of the two issues should help students know (1) that Jewish immigrants might be torn between a desire to "be American" and an obligation to preserve their heritage; (2) that anti-Semitism, which may have economic and political as well as religious bases, is manifestly in opposition to the ideals of both Christianity and American democracy; and (3) that anti-Jewish discrimination can be eliminated only through the understanding and cooperation of all Americans.

Americanization

When discussing Americanization, the following should be considered.

1. According to Rabbi Wise, why must a Jew become an American?

Becoming an American meant throwing off the old attitudes, getting rid of traditional "hang-ups." If the Jew did not do this, he would be denying himself the opportunity to reap the American harvest to the fullest. The best way to do this, said Wise, was to break with the Old World and help shape a New World.

2. What might a German Jewish immigrant do to become Americanized?

To become an American the Jew must shed those thought patterns and modes of behavior which would mark him as European or German. The Jew, where no real question of principle was involved, should adopt American speech and clothing, and should join in wider recreational and social relationships. He should take his place beside other Americans in the mainstream of life, not retreat into the familiar security of a self-made ghetto. Rabbi Wise did not argue for a surrender of Jewishness, but of "Germanness" that unnecessarily set apart the immigrants of his generation.

3. As Rabbi Schechter speaks of the Jews' "glorious heritage" and the Torah, he reveals his real concern with Americanization. To what is he primarily opposed?

Rabbi Schechter was concerned that Jews would trade away essential elements of Judaism. He felt that Jews did not have to compromise their religion to achieve civil liberties, or to receive the blessings of America, or to contribute to the nation's welfare.

4. What place, says Schechter, should the institutions and laws of Judaism hold?

Schechter felt that the institutions, laws, and observances of Judaism were of critical importance. He took this position at a time when some Jewish leaders were advocating the abandonment of what they felt were the non-essential and out-moded trappings of religion.

5. What had Nativists implied that Catholics should give up? Could you say, then, that Jews and Catholics were being asked to pay the same price for Americanization? If so, what was it?

Nativists had demanded that Catholics give up loyalty to the Pope and to their Universal Church. In the case of the Jews the demand was often expressed in impatience with ethnic peculiarities, linguistic diversity, and political nonconformity. Sometimes, however, the pressure for conversion to Christianity was also great. In effect, then, both Catholic and Jew were being asked—by some—to surrender major portions of their own religious heritage. And this request came in a nation made up of various religious heritages and traditions.

Anti-Semitism

As you discuss anti-Semitism, the following should be considered.

1. Why is anti-Semitism fundamentally anti-Christian?

The hatred of the anti-Semite directly contradicts the love ethic of Christianity. Prejudice strikes at the foundations of a common brotherhood derived from a single Fatherhood. Therefore, anti-Semitism is a denial of the Christian view of both human and divine relationships.

2. Rabbi Gilbert notes that anti-Semites allude to the threat of "Jewish bankers" and "Jewish Communists."

    a. If an anti-Semite warned of the above, would his charge be self-contradictory? Why? Why not?
    b. To whom might the "bankers'" charge appeal? To whom might the "Communists'" charge appeal?

The beliefs that "Jews control the business world and are only interested in profit-making" and that "Jews are usually radical and socialist" (Communist, too) constitute a contradiction that rarely bothers the anti-Semite. He will criticize Jewish capitalism, but not capitalism. He will praise hard work and success in business except when the hardworking, successful businessman is a Jew. The charge that Jews control business appeals to the "have nots" and the "would haves" in a society that can use the Jews (as a group) as its whipping-boy. Likewise, "Communism" can be the excuse for all of one's own failures and society's ills.

Students should be helped, in the discussion, to see the irrational and contradictory nature of such charges. Recognition of logical inconsistency is a first step toward abandonment of stereotypes.

3. Both religious and racial anti-Semitism are referred to. What do these modifiers mean? What other types might exist? To whom would these types appeal?

Anti-Semitism appeals to many persons who also harbor prejudices against the Negro, Oriental, Catholic, or "foreigner." Highly prejudiced people, often called "bigots," sometimes have singular personality traits that help explain their biases. Individuals who have experienced frustration or rejection may have difficulty in understanding the complexities of society. They may look around for an easy explanation of their difficulties. The explanation often lies with "others"—those of another group. People may be classified as "we" (who are good) and "they" (who are evil). Sometimes the "they" is ill-defined. But other times a recognizable ethnic or religious group well serves as the "they." As a minority group often displaying superior ability, Jews have been the "they" in many societies, in many centuries.

Religious anti-Semitism stems from Christian doctrine, the main theme being (1) The diaspora as God's scattering of the Jews as punishment for the Crucifixion; (2) the "degenerate state" of Judaism in the time of Jesus, and (3) the crime of deicide.[1] Ethnocentrism is common to human groups the world over. Usually, though, it is based upon cultural differences, not biological differences. In the nineteenth century race and nationality began to be confused and some races were said to be superior. This supposed superiority (especially in a natural ability to rule) was used to justify imperialistic ventures. When Germans were lauded as superior racial types, the Jews in their midst became an inferior race. The horrors of Nazi Germany were manifestations of racist philosophy. America, too, thought in terms of superior "stocks" in the restrictive immigration law of 1924.

Anti-Semitism may be <u>political</u>: "The Jews want power." It may be <u>economic</u>: "They control all the businesses." It may be <u>cultural</u>: "The Jews don't act like we do." All these ways of fostering resentment, and others as well, may be added to the racial-religious biases noted above.[2]

---

[1] See Isaac, <u>The Teaching of Contempt</u> in the student volume. Also see Arthur Gilbert, <u>The Vatican Council and the Jews</u> (Cleveland: World Publishing Company, 1968).

[2] For further treatment, see Hunt, Maurice P. and Laurence E. Metcalf. <u>Teaching High School Social Studies.</u> Chapter 18 "Problematic Areas of Culture: Race and Minority Group Relations," New York, 1968.

4. According to Gilbert's quote from H. A. Overstreet, of what are too many Americans guilty? Explain.

Too many Americans are passive concerning anti-Semitism. They let it exist. By not speaking out against anti-Semitism many Americans are guilty of aiding the anti-Semite. Also, by their own behavior some people show that they think of Jews differently than they do of other Americans. This behavior creates a social situation in which the aggressive anti-Semite is encouraged.

5. Following Overstreet's hints, how can Americans eliminate anti-Semitism?

Americans must examine their own attitudes and behavior to see if they harbor traces of anti-Semitism, traces which help create a social sanction for prejudice. When people awake to their own role in fostering anti-Semitism, they should then consciously strive to change their own behavior. With this done, the chances of eliminating anti-Semitism will be increased.

Jews and Judaism

1. How do you understand the expression "Religious civilization"?

Students are asked to reflect upon the difference between a "religion" and a "religious civilization" and Kaplan offers a line which will help students in discussion make a distinction: "If Judaism is to mean that which unites Jews into an identifiable and distinct group. . . ."

2. What three contemporary problems does Kaplan hope to solve for American Jews?

a) The sense of identity of today's Jews with past generations, b) the interpretation of tradition to make it compatible with naturalism and the ethical conception of nationalism, and c) the accommodation of Jewish diversity with the survival of Jewish life and its influence upon human life in general.

3. Judging from the passage given here, what are some of the "universal human values" you would expect Kaplan to support?

Students are asked to make inferences from this brief passage. In the class discussion, the teacher might help students explore these possibilities in relation to Kaplan's position: "justice," "equality," "the dignity of the individual personality," "religious and civil liberty," "cooperation of men," "one's own cultural traditions," and "pluralism."

EASTERN ORTHODOXY IN AMERICA

Eastern Orthodoxy is America's fourth largest religious group. Many of the problems of Americanization experienced by earlier immigrants faced the Orthodox faithful in the twentieth century. How to preserve religious institutions and still enter the mainstream of American life proved difficult for many. Fortunately Eastern Orthodox immigrants have generally been spared the vigorous opposition of the Nativist and the anti-Semite.

The student text presents an overview of Orthodoxy in America and then focuses upon a phenomenon of central concern to all American religious groups. The ecumenical movement—a move toward cooperation and even unity—among Christian churches has forced churchmen to inquire into their traditional relationship with other religious groups. Such inquiry often involves questioning the relevance or importance of doctrines, practices, and institutions. Within a single denomination, as well as among the several denominations, concerned clergy and laity have taken a variety of positions on the ecumenical movement. The stances of the two eminent Orthodox leaders reflect a typical "line-up" on the ecumenical question.

When discussing Eastern Orthodoxy and ecumenism the following should be considered.

1. Why would the question of relations with other churches be a "new" problem to most Orthodox immigrants?

Most Orthodox immigrants did not come from countries where religious pluralism existed. In many cases, Orthodoxy was the established or state religion. This was true in Russia until 1917. Members of other religions such as Jews or Roman Catholics often suffered political or social disabilities. In other countries the Orthodox church was relegated to an inferior status. This was true in the Ottoman Empire. In still other countries, such as Yugoslavia, conflict between adherents to Eastern Orthodoxy and Western Catholicism was common. In all these cases cooperation among religious groups was certainly the exception—not the rule.

2. What is the central theme of Archbishop Iakovos' message? To whom is he addressing this message? Why?

Archbishop Iakovas states that church unity can be realized only if individual Christians commit themselves to it. It is a mission that "Christians have been assigned to fulfill." "The least we can do is to see and understand church unity as a Divine Call, as a sacred duty and as the fulfillment of the gospel itself, of which we must be the servants."

Iakovos' sermon is addressed to more than those in St. Patrick's Cathedral. He is calling upon all Christians to find the true meaning in unity, and to work for that unity. Iakovos knows that the efforts of church leaders and organizations are not enough to bring real unity. Christian unity can come only from the hearts of men.

3. What is the basic argument of Metropolitan Philaret? Why does he oppose cooperation among different churches (i.e., ecumenism)? What role does "canon law" play? (You may want to consult an encyclopedia on the meaning of canon law.)

Philaret argues that the participation by Iakovos in ecumenical ventures is entirely out of order. Iakovos, he says, is violating church canons. He is rejecting the teachings (as is Patriarch Athenagoras) of the Holy Fathers. This activity of Iakovos only serves to confuse the faithful and mislead "those who are 'without'."

Philaret opposes these ecumenical ventures because he sees this as compromising the Church. His position is that the Orthodox is the "only One Holy, Catholic and Apostolic Church. . . ." The Christian task of the faithful should be to bring the heterodox into the church, not to compromise with them. The Metropolitan refers to traditions and divine dogmas (unalterable truths from God) which cannot be compromised.

4. Do you feel that Iakovos anticipated the criticism of Philaret? If so, how?

Archbishop Iakovos was aware of the opposition to efforts at church unity. He notes that "We do not like even for the sake of Christ to reexamine our own confessional traditions and disciplines." Also, his definition of church unity (from St. Epiphanius of Cyprus) seems to obviate the arguments of those opposing church unity.

5. Could one say that Philaret and Rabbi Schechter share concerns? Why? Why not?

Philaret and Rabbi Schechter were both concerned lest vital elements of their faiths be compromised, thus changing the nature of ther religious traditions. Philaret sees value in the traditions set down by the church fathers; Schechter sees values in Judaism's "glorious heritage." Both are concerned about what might be lost, not so much about what might be gained.

The two situations differ, however. Schechter favors Americanization; he feels that Jews can "be American" and still retain the traditional institutions of faith. Philaret does not favor ecumenism; he sees this movement as incompatible with Orthodoxy. Thus do Philaret and Schechter take different stances with respect to the issue each faces.

6. How is the "dialogue" of Iakovos and Philaret illustrative of the problems facing other American churches? Can you give any examples?

The Eastern Orthodox family is not the only one beset by dissent over questions of church cooperation. Various Protestant proposals of mergers in America have provoked disagreement among clergy and laity. Some proposals have been rejected or delayed, while others have been approved. Examples of the latter include the reunion of northern and southern Methodists in 1939, the joining of the Evangelical and Reformed Church with the Congregationalists in 1957, and the formation in 1962 of the Lutheran Church in America out of several smaller bodies. Since 1962, the Consultation on Church Union has brought together a number of Protestant bodies—including Methodist, Episcopal, Presbyterian, Disciples, and the United Church of Christ—to discuss possible church union. Some large Protestant groups—such as the Baptists and Lutherans—are not involved in the Consultation on Church Union. So a variety of positions on church unity can be seen here as well as in the confrontation between Archbishop Iakovos and Metropolitan Philaret. Serious theological and philosophical differences—as well as historical and cultural considerations—often obstruct moves toward unity among Protestants. Obviously the difficulties multiply when Protestants and Orthodox and Roman Catholics all talk of a common church.

PATTERNS OF PLURALISM

America's pluralistic religious community presents a confusing picture to those contemplating it. In this section of the study the picture is clarified for students. Information is presented in the form of statistical charts. The primary purpose of this section is to have students (1) know the size and division of America's religious population and (2) relate this information to previous learnings in order to make generalizations about the development of the present pattern of pluralism. Discussion of this section should be brief and should "set the stage" for the next section, which looks at the problems of religious pluralism in modern America.

When discussing the patterns of pluralism the following should be considered.

1. What percentage of the <u>national population</u> is Protestant? Catholic? Jewish? Eastern Orthodox?

The Protestant families (including Latter-Day Saints) comprise 32.5% of the national population. Roman Catholics comprise 23.8%; Jewish, 2.9%; and Eastern Orthodox, 1.6%. (Note: a proliferation of small Protestant bodies exist which would make the total Protestant percentage slightly higher. Also, note that the Jewish figure is one of population, not of synagogue membership. Probably about one-half of America's Jews are "observant Jews"—that is, participants in the institutional forms of Judaism. Students should understand that "Jews in America" and "Judaism in America" are not equivalent expressions.)

2. What percentage of total church membership do these groups comprise?

The Protestant comprise 50.4% of America's religious population. Catholics comprise 37.1%; Jews 4.5%; and Eastern Orthodox 2.5%.

3. Compare this information with Table I.

   a. What does this tell us about the "success" of nativism?

   b. What generalizations could you make about the growth of the various denominations? What might account for the great changes in proportional strength?

Nativism obviously failed to keep America's religious pattern the same that it was around 1850. Table I showed us that in 1820 American churches were almost all Protestant. However, Figure 3 shows us that in 1965 Protestants accounted for just one-half (50.4%) of the religious population of the United States. Furthermore, Table II revealed that of the national population Protestantism could claim but 32.5%. Thus, while Nativists might have once claimed that America was a Protestant nation, the claim is certainly not valid today. (It should be pointed out, however, that the figures used are actual church affiliation. There are many other Americans who may "feel" that they are Protestants or Catholics.)

Students should be encouraged to speculate about the reasons for the changes in America's religious pattern. They should consider colonial backgrounds, immigration, the nature of American liberty, patterns of settlement in the West, evangelical effectiveness, social prestige, doctrinal distinctives, etc.

PROBLEMS OF PLURALISM

After tracing the course of America's religious pluralism, examining the issues accompanying its growth, and surveying its present pattern, we now turn to an investigation of the meaning of pluralism. What problems does pluralism present for religion today? What problems does pluralism hold for the future of religion in America? In this section we shall explore these vital considerations.

Students are provided only one reading in this section: Religion and American Society, which serves as the basis of class discussion. While some of our inquiries may be answered directly from this text, the discussion questions will require students to apply all they may know about religion and society. This "in depth" discussion may well raise more issues than it settles, which is as it should be. There are no pat answers to the persisting problems raised by the authors. Neither should you expect agreement among the students on the framing of the problem or on their suggested resolution. American churchmen don't all agree, so there is no reason why students should!

Emphasis in the discussion should be placed on having students (1) understand the problems as framed by the authors, (2) determine the sources of the problems, (3) offer and support possible resolutions of the problems. Since some students may have difficulty comprehending the reading, you can precede the discussion with a "directed study" period in which individual help is given. The discussion may then begin with a "clarification" of the reading prior to taking up the five questions.

The following points may be made in the discussion, but students should be encouraged to offer alternatives and additions.

1. What effect may the "openness" of American society have on an individual's religious beliefs? What, in turn, might this do to the character of religion in America?

Since the notion that "the majority is right" (rather than "the majority prevails") is ingrained in most Americans, there is a tendency to try to make religion "fit" the majority. Also, because today's majority may be tomorrow's minority, one may view many beliefs, including religious beliefs, as less than fundamental or enduring. These tendencies could make American religion an innocuous thing, providing some solace or security or fellowship, but little vitality or sense of direction. Compromise in political and social dealings preserves group harmony and unity. Compromise in moral principles and religious loyalty undermines the integrity of both individual and group.

2. Does the slogan, "It doesn't matter what you believe, as long as you're sincere," have relevance to this reading? Why? Why not?

The slogan has much relevance here. The authors note the "unhealthy assumption that all positions either are all on a plane and do not matter one way or the other or are wholly matters of taste and background." The "live and let live" attitude carried to the extreme brings us full circle to the "dog eat dog" rule of the jungle.

Historically, religion has provided many people with guidelines for living. For others, adequate bases are derived from nonreligious sources. In either event, the power of ideas is such that they may shape the kind of life one leads. And that is a difference of some magnitude.

3. The authors state that "sanctions for churchgoing are significantly a matter for social approval. . . ." What effect might this have on the quality of religion?

If the "sanctions for churchgoing are significantly a matter of social approval," religion has become a tool of other social institutions. Religious institutions and practices then merely reflect the secular society. Religion thus becomes powerless and passive. People may affiliate with a church and perform the rituals, thereby winning social approval. But when the basic teachings of the synagogue or church go unheeded, then these institutions, in the words of Rabbi Stephen Wise, become "forces of respectability" rather than "forces of righteousness."

4. Why shouldn't theological unbelief be looked upon as a democratic heresy or political disloyalty?

When theological unbelief is looked upon as a democratic heresy or political disloyalty, religion is, again, a utensil serving secular institutions. In this case the institution is a deified state. Some may seek to demonstrate their "Americanism" by paying lip service to faith in God. This is, of course, not religious commitment, but a perversion of it. Citizens regard religion as a mere adjunct of political philosophy or a proof of political loyalty, then religion is only a "patriotic exercise," a "meaningless nationalistic ritual." A "common creed" may foster group harmony, but it may at the same time destroy liberty of conscience and personal worth.

5. What do the authors mean by religion becoming a "victim of society" rather than a "judge of society"?

From the above, it follows that religion can become a "victim of society" rather than a "judge of society." The servant cannot judge the master. And, the master will not heed the servant.

A society needs a critic, just as an individual does. Neither persons nor national powers can be placed beyond all reproof or correction—laws unto themselves. The state which assumes an absolute or infallible character becomes tyrannical and despotic. One of democracy's surest protectors, therefore, is the voice of religion, reminding the state of its finiteness, of its limitations, of its self-imposed restraints. Whenever a political society aspires to be totalitarian, it attacks religion. For totalitarianism cannot endure a competing loyalty, nor can it accept the premise that the sanctity of the individual has precedence over the prerogatives of the state.

CONTEMPORARY PARALLEL

When the Supreme Court ruled against Bible-reading and the Lord's Prayer as devotional exercises in public schools (1963), Senator Strom Thurmond expressed the sentiment of many citizens when he called the decision "another major triumph for the forces of secularism and atheism." The public uproar over that decision and the continued attempts to ignore, subvert, or nullify the ruling present an interesting contemporary parallel to the problems that a pluralistic society has in adjusting to the different religious convictions of its citizens.

Can students find evidence of the "Godless public schools" sentiment in their community? Is there local controversy over such things as school devotionals, religious assembly programs, Christmas observances, or Baccalaureate services? Does the local school board have guidelines in this area? Assignments to study key Court decisions involving religion and the public schools would be an appropriate way of exposing students to the important issues. Such cases would include Everson (1947), dealing with public funds for bus transportation of children attending Roman Catholic parochial schools; McCollum (1948), relating to "released time" programs involving the use of public school buildings for various religious groups; Zorach (1952), a further interpretation of "released time" programs; Engel (1962), relating to the use of a State-sponsored prayer in the public schools of New York; and Schempp (1963), dealing with the reading of the Bible and the Lord's Prayer as part of daily religious exercises in the public schools.

Another valuable area for exploration is the efforts being made to incorporate the study about religion in the public schools' curricula as "part of a secular program of education." The Reader's Guide to Periodical Literature lists articles on the subject, which will support student inquiry.

SUGGESTED ACTIVITIES

Because discussion is used throughout this study, this section emphasizes written assignments. Activities 1 or 2, one of which should be mandatory for all students, ought to be shared with the class upon completion.

1. Essay

Read once more the first paragraph of the selection from Religion and American Society. How can the existence of unavoidable tension between Judaeo-Christian faith and secular society help explain the Americanization dilemma faced by:

    a. Roman Catholics in mid-nineteenth century
    b. Jews in late nineteenth century
    c. Eastern Orthodox in mid-twentieth

This essay is designed for average to above average students. It does not demand additional reading. Students are asked to apply the thesis of the authors of Religion and American Society to the three immigrant experiences. They should read the authors' paragraph on "tension" very carefully. Every phrase in that paragraph can be illustrated in the readings on America's Catholics, Jews, and Orthodox.

2. List

What events in American history and what contemporary issues illustrate the unavoidable tensions between Judaeo-Christian faith and secular society? Compile a list of these events and issues. Be able to explain why each is an example of the tension as defined by the authors of Religion and American Society.

The list is designed for average or below average students. Much teacher direction should be given as students will require other sources of information. The school library should be fully utilized. When the list of events and issues is compiled, help students explain how each is an example of the tensions defined by the authors. Some possible examples for the list are:

    The Scopes Trial evolution-teaching controversy
    Jehovah's Witness flag salute controversy
    Government birth control programs
    Conscientious objection to the draft
    Amish refusal to send children to school
    Suits against school prayer
    Parents refusing medical treatment for children
    The closing of liquor stores on Sunday

3. Library Paper

The library paper should be undertaken only by superior students. They should begin work on it early in the study as two weeks should be allotted for its completion. Information provided in the student text should serve as a starting point for the investigation. The library paper should include an explanation of the "melting pot" and cultural "pluralism" theories and how well each of these fits the American scene. Hypotheses regarding the role of religion vis-a-vis other factors should be offered in determining that America should be "pluralist" rather than a "melting pot."

In the late nineteenth and early twentieth centuries, American social philosophers spoke of the United States as the great "melting pot." More recently social philosophers talk of "cultural pluralism." Investigate the reasons for this change in labels. What role does religion play, if any, in this change of labels? Were other factors more or less important than religion?

Suggestions for Further Research

These areas of investigation are suggested for those students wishing to do additional research. In guiding students in their individual efforts, be sure to use the "Basic Library" as well as the Resource Guide below.

    a. The Ecumenical Movement in America
       1) What is it? How or when did it start?
       2) What are the principal mergers of the twentieth century?
       3) What are the major arguments for or against church union? (You may explain the position of a single group, if you wish.)

b. The Jewish Community
   1) Who are America's Jews?
   2) What are the divisions of American Judaism?
   3) What is the relationship between Jewish and Christian bodies?
   4) What is the relationship between American Jewry and Israel?
   5) What can you discover about the National Conference of Christians and Jews?

VOCABULARY

acquiesce	eschelon	irreconcilable	refute
adherent	ethnic	mandatory	sanction
affirm	exhortation	ostracism	sanctuary
assimilation	extirpate	paradox	solicitude
aver	fanaticism	pernicious	sovereignty
avow, disavow	ghetto	pragmatic	subversive
bigot	gullibility	precedent	tangible, intangible
canon	harangue	propagate	temporal
desecration	influx	prudent	transcend
diametric	iota	quota	virulent
efface			

RESOURCE GUIDE FOR STUDY 10

I. Audio Visual Aids

A. Films

An American Girl. 29 min., b&w, rental: Service Charge
   Anti-Defamation League, 315 Lexington Ave., New York, N.Y. 10016
Anti-Semitism appears when a Gentile girl begins wearing a "Jewish" bracelet.

The American Jew: A Tribute to Freedom. 45 min., b&w, rental: Service Charge
   Anti-Defamation League, 315 Lexington Ave., New York, N.Y. 10016
An historical look at the contribution of Jews to America.

Belonging to the Group. 16 min., b&w, rental $3.50
   Encyclopedia Britannica Film, 425 N. Michigan Ave., Chicago, Ill. 60611
This film explores the problem facing new comers to a community.

Boundary Lines. 11 min., rental $5.00
   International Film Foundation, 475 Fifth Ave., New York, N.Y. 10017
Through the use of animated symbolic art, music, sound effects and serious commentary, this film dramatizes the boundary lines of fear, greed, and insecurity which separate people from one another. A fine study of prejudice, this film could well introduce the study.

Can We Immunize Against Prejudice? 7 min., b&w, rental: rates vary
   Columbia University Press Center for Mass Communications, 1125 Amsterdam Ave., New York, N.Y. 10025
In a semi-cartoon manner, the film explores the methods for immunizing children against infection by prejudice.

The Chosen People. 27 min., rental $7.50
  Produced by NBC–TV. Available from Anti-Defamation League, 315 Lexington Ave., New York, N.Y. 10016
In this film high school students discover that anti-Semitism exists in their own community. The individual's responsibility regarding prejudice is explored. This would supplement nicely the readings on anti-Semitism.

A Day in the Night of Jonathan Mole. 32 min., b&w, rental $4.00
  National Film Board of Canada. Available from Contemporary Films, 267 W. 25th Street, New York, N.Y. 10001
Fantasy courtroom trial explores bias and prejudice—an Indian, a Jew and an immigrant are the "defendants." This film could very well introduce the study.

Dr. Louis Finkelstein. 26 min., rental $5.50
  Encyclopedia Britannica Film Library, 425 N. Michigan Ave., Chicago, Illinois 60611
Dr. Finkelstein, Chancellor of the Jewish Theological Seminary of America, discusses the spiritual problems of the American people.

The Golden Door. 15 min., color, rental: Apply
  Church World Service, 475 Riverside Drive, New York, N.Y. 10027
This film describes immigration, past and present. Also, it calls for improving immigration laws.

The Great Conversation. 54 min., rental: varies
  Produced by ABC–TV, available from many university and educational film libraries, plus some denominational libraries.
This film explores the ecumenical movement in Christianity. It analyzes the trends toward reconciliation and reports on the action of ecumenists in many countries. This film could well follow the readings on Eastern Orthodoxy.

Harvest of Shame. 54 min., b&w, rental: rates vary
  CBS–TV, 51 W. 52nd St., New York, N.Y. 10019
The plight of the migrant worker is explored. The role of the churches in alleviating the situation is raised.

Ku Klux Klan: The Invisible Empire. 47 min., b&w, rental: rates vary
  Carousel Film Libraries, 1501 Broadway, New York, N.Y. 10036
Microphones and on-the-spot cameras document this news report of the history, viewpoints and practices of the KKK.

The Lady from Philadelphia. 58 min., rental $25.00
  Contemporary Films, 257 W. 25th St., New York, N.Y. 10001
This film documents Marian Anderson's tour of Southeast Asia. It features the performance of songs and brief statements on religion and citizenship.

The Old Order Amish. 33 min., rental $10.00
  Vedo Films, 85 Longview Rd., Port Washington, New York 11050
Presents Amish religion and society and their efforts to maintain traditional ways. This raises question of "Americanization" vs. tradition. (Highly recommended.)

One God. 37 min., rental $12.50
   Anti-Defamation League, 315 Lexington Ave., New York, N.Y. 10016
This film presents major worship forms of Protestants, Catholics and Jews in the U.S. (Highly recommended.)

Our Immigrant Heritage. 32 min., color, rental $10.60
   McGraw-Hill (Text-film Dept.), 330 W. 42nd St., New York, N.Y. 10036
The film examines the variety of cultural traditions which influence modern America. It includes treatment of the nativists, Know-Nothings, KKK, who opposed immigration.

The Tourist. 30 min., b&w, rental: $8.00
   The Methodist Church, 201 Eighth Ave., S. Nashville, Tenn. (Also available from many regional centers.)
Explores how people react to the plight of foreigners new to the country.

What About Prejudice? 12 min., rental: varies
   McGraw-Hill (Text-film Dept.), 330 W. 42nd St., New York, N. Y. 10036
This film examines the damage that prejudice can do to a high school student and shows how prejudice is passed from parent to child. This could initiate the study.

Where is Prejudice? b&w, rental: $10.15
   Audio Visual Center, Circulation Dept., Indiana University, Bloomington, Indiana 47401
Twelve students of different racial and religious backgrounds test their own conviction that they were not prejudiced.

B. Film Strips

   Ask the Brave Soldier. 94-frames, b&W, sale: $8.00
      National Conference of Christians and Jews, 43 W. 57th St., New York, N. Y. 10019
   This filmstrip explores problems of human relations on the neighborhood level.

C. Recordings
      Divine Liturgy of St. John Chrysostom. Afonsky-New York Orthodox Cathedral Choir.
         Westminster Records WST-14204 Price $4.95

      Russian Orthodox Requiem. Afonsky—A Capella-Russian Male Chorus.
         Westminster Records WST-14263 Price $4.98

D. Miscellaneous

   Kit of Jewish Religious Articles. sale $10.00
      Anti-Defamation League, 315 Lexington Ave., New York, N.Y. 10016
   (Contains: 10 artifacts, descriptive pamphlets and a guide to the use of the artifacts in preaching and teaching.)

   Map: Makers of the U.S.A. (40" x 30", $1.00; 13½" x 11", $.50 a dozen)
      Shows the many nationalities, cultures and races that make up the U.S.A. Available from the Broadcasting and Film Commission, National Council of Churches, 475 Riverside Drive, New York, N. Y. 10027

II. Articles

"Danger Ahead" For the American Catholic Church, America, vol. 119 (November 16, 1968).

"Hooded Horsemen Gallop Out of the Past in a Sudden Revival of the KKK," Life, vol. 58 (April 23, 1965).

"How U.S. Catholics View Their Church: Major Findings of Survey," Newsweek, vol. 69 (March 20, 1967).

"Jews and Christians in Suburbia," Harper, vol. 235 (August, 1967).

"Is Ecumenism Running Out of Fuel?" Christianity Today, vol. 12 (March 1, 1968).
A critical look at the ecumenical movement.

"Methodism and Ecumenism: A New Flexibility," Christian Century, vol. 85 (April 3, 1968).

"Mexican-Americans Make Themselves Heard," Reporter, vol. 36 (February 9, 1967).

"Interaction in the Adopted Land: Exploring the Jewish Experience in America," Saturday Review, vol. 51 (December 7, 1968).

"Intergroup Relations in Religious Textbooks." Reprinted from Religious Education, vol. 55 (March–April 1960). New York: American Jewish Committee. $.25

"O Blessed Deviation," Commonweal, vol. 86 (June 16, 1967).

"Once More the KKK," New York Times Magazine (August 11, 1963).

"Plea for Unity," U.S. News and World Report, vol. 112 (May 9, 1966).

"Pocho's Progress: Nation's Second Largest Disadvantaged Minority," Time, vol. 89 (April 28, 1967).

"Road Between Rome and Jerusalem," Saturday Review, vol. 49 (December 3, 1966).

"Unity Week? Belated Entry of Roman Catholics," Newsweek, vol. 71 (February 5, 1968).

"What Church Unity Demands of Catholics and Protestants," Redbook, vol. 126 (March, 1966).

III. Books

Abbott, Walter M., S.J. (ed.). Documents of Vatican II. Washington, D.C.: Guild Press. (paper) $1.45, New York: Association Press. (paper) $1.45

Billington, Ray A. Protestant Crusade: 1800–1860. Chicago: Quadrangle Books. (paper) $2.95

Blau, Joseph L. Modern Varieties of Judaism. New York: Columbia University Press. $7.50

Callinikos, C. The History of the Orthodox Church. Divrey Publications. $1.00

Commentary. The Condition of Jewish Belief: A Symposium. New York: Macmillan. (paper) $1.45

Coniaris, Anthony. Eastern Orthodoxy: A Way of Life. Bangor, Maine: American Orthodox Press, $3.95

Constantelos, Demetrios J. The Greek Orthodox Church. New York: Seabury Press. $1.95

Davis, Moshe. The Emergence of Conservative Judaism. Philadelphia: Jewish Publication Society of America. $5.50

Dunne, J. G. Delano: The Story of the California Grape Strike.

Glock, Charles Y., and Stark, Rodney. Christian Beliefs and Anti-Semitism: A Scientific Study of the Ways in Which the Teachings of Christian Churches Shapes American Attitudes Toward the Jews. New York: Harper and Row. (text ed.) $1.95

Gordis, Robert. Judaism for the Modern Age. New York: Farrar, Strauss, and Cudahy. $4.50

Greeley, Andrew M. The Catholic Experience: An Interpretation of the History of American Catholicism. Garden City, New York: Doubleday (Image) (paper) $1.25

Harstein, Jacob (ed.). The Jews in American History: A Resource Book for the Teacher of Social Studies and American History. Anti-Defamation League of B'nai B'rith. $1.50

Hertzberg, Arthur (editor). Judaism. New York: Braziller. $4.00

Hobson, Laura A. Gentleman's Agreement. New York: Avon. (paper) $.75

Lanternari, Vittorio. Religions of the Oppressed. New York: New American Library (paper) $.75

Liebman, Charles S. Orthodoxy in American Jewish Life. Reprinted from American Jewish Year Book, vol. 66, 1965. New York: American Jewish Committee. $.75

Mandelbaum, Seymour. Social Setting of Intolerance: the Know-Nothings, The Red Scare, and McCarthyism. Glenview, Illinois: Scott, Foresman (paper) $1.96

Menkus, Belden (ed.). Meet the American Jew. Nashville: Broadman Press (paper) $1.25

Newcomb, Covelle. Larger than the Sky: The Story of James Cardinal Gibbons. New York: McKay. $4.50

Potok, Chaim. The Chosen. New York: Fawcett World Library. (paper) $.95

Rouse, Ruth and Stephen C. Neill. A History of the Ecumenical Movement. 2nd ed. Philadelphia: Westminster Press. $10.00

St. John, Robert. Jews, Justice and Judaism: A Narrative of the Role by the Bible People in Shaping American History. Garden City, New York: Doubleday. $6.95

Stephanou, E. Belief and Practices in the Orthodox Church. Divney Publication, $1.50

IV. Pamphlets

Feldman, Abraham J. Contributions of Judaism to Modern Society. (available from the Commission on Information About Judaism, 838 Fifth Avenue, New York, N. Y. 10021.)

Handlin, Oscar. American Jews: Their Story. Anti-Defamation League. $.50

_____. American Jews: Their Story (Teacher's Guide) Anti-Defamation League. $.35

_____ and Mary. Danger in Discord. Anti-Defamation League.

_____. Out of Many: A Study Guide to Cultural Pluralism in the United States. Anti-Defamation League. $.35

Religion and American Society. Center for the Study of Democratic Institutions. Santa Barbara, California, 1961.

The Churches and the Public. Center for the Study of Democratic Institutions. Santa Barbara, 1960.

Religion and the Free Society. Center for the Study of Democratic Institutions. New York, 1958.

Religion and the Schools. Center for the Study of Democratic Institutions. New York, 1959.

(In the Basic Library, particular attention is called to the following volumes:

Braden, These Also Believe

Clark, The Small Sects in America

Ellis, American Catholicism

Glazer, American Judaism

Hudson, American Protestantism

McLoughlin and Bellah, Religion in America

Yearbook of American Churches)